JANE

I've been in a relationship with this guy for 4 years going to 5 years now. He told me about marriage the very first time he came but I asked him to wait after my schooling because I actually thought he is one of those people who come to use marriage to get their way and also because of my past experience.We started dating and he was really supportive during my school days..I'm done with school and just Passed out recently from National Youth Service and now he wants to proceed with the marriage plans but I'm no longer interested.

Reason is, since our years of dating this guy has really been struggling financially, with no steady source of income. Today he has money, tomorrow he is so broke that he has to struggle so much to feed and pay his rent. Even the business we started together went down the drain cause he kept borrowing from it without paying back.

I have siblings to cater for as the first child and daughter, I don't want a marriage. My life as a single will be better/preferred than life in marriage judging from his financial condition from the past years. Ma I might sound selfish but this is my greatest fear. Aside from this, he is really a good man but what becomes of us after the wedding? I'm scared my future is not guaranteed with him and I've tried talking to him about setting up a business first before we start the marriage process so we can have what to fall back on after the wedding.

I'm not going to sit idle, I'll surely get a job but I wouldn't want to get into a marriage. I'll be the sole breadwinner when I have a husband.

I don't know if I'm overthinking or overreacting to this issue.

IMAOBONG

We did not date. Though we had known each other as church members for some years, we were not close. I was in my late thirties and the pressure was high for me to get married. It wasn't like I was not getting approached by men, I just did not see what I wanted in them. I guess it was the same for my husband because I never had any interest in him. He was just a regular church brother.

When my pastor's wife approached me about the possibility of getting married to him, I outrightly told her "No" but she insisted I think about it. I didn't know they already mentioned it to him too. My pastor's wife kept talking to me about it. Soon my pastor joined too and in fact called us both into a meeting. We were told they had prayed about it and they have a conviction it's God's will. My husband was very willing, I was skeptical but because I trusted my pastor's judgment, I finally accepted.

We started the marriage plans almost immediately and in 6 months, we were married. It wasn't the kind of marriage I wanted, there was no love and barely any friendship. It was more like two people cohabiting and just being nice to each other. Even sex wasn't enjoyable. One year turned into 2 and then 5 but there was no child. It made the relationship worse. My husband did not have a fixed job so I bore most of our financial burdens. He started staying away from the home more often and I suspected him of cheating too.

It wasn't long before I was proved right. He told me another lady was pregnant for him. I was hurt and angry but what could I do? He moved out and I was left alone. The only good thing about the marriage is that I am good with his family. I still visit them to spend time with his mother. She tries to console me about my childlessness and her son's behavior but she can't fault him. She too wants grandchildren.

Last year though, we started talking again. Though he hasn't moved back to the house, he comes around and when I visit his mum in the village, he also shows up. I regret the marriage but divorce is not an option for me. I do not blame my pastor either because I'm sure they only wanted the best for us and would not have known the marriage would turn out this way. Besides, I should have stood my ground when I knew it wasn't what I wanted.

Last year, I took in a young relative and she has been the one that has relieved me of loneliness and made me a mother. I spend my time now between work, church and taking care of myself and her.

NECHE

"I met him 7 years ago, at my place of work. As at then, I was serving in a restaurant. I had served him and his friends when they came to eat and the moment he saw me he told me straight up, " I like you, I am married,but,I want to make you my second wife." I didn't think he was serious and waved it aside.

Weeks later,he came back and met my boss telling her to talk to me about marrying him. From his persistence, I accepted to date him.

Though I didn't see any future with him because of the age difference. I was 20 and he was 34 when we met. I accepted because at the time he came, I really needed someone to lean on financially and he was rich.

Before you judge me, just know that I have gone through a lot as an oprhan. I have felt pain, seen hunger and know what starvation is.

I have been mistreated, molested, harassed and abused as a child. Catering for myself as a child wasn't what I'dwish my enemies. I have gone through hell so much that my pillow has been my best friend. I watched the people that were supposed to protect me turn their back on me. I was just a girl that needed to survive.

2 months into our relationship, I noticed there was hardly any communication with his wife as they lived in different states. He told me he was having issues with her which was later resolved after much pleading by me.

I threatened to leave if he did not resolve his issues with his wife. Other than that, I also noticed some other red flags as early as few days into the relationship.

I was living with my boss then and we were more like a family. But the moment I started dating him, he changed how I related with them.

He would accuse me of sleeping with the woman's son. He deleted every picture I took with him even when he knew I took him as my brother. He would demand video calls to prove where I was at every time, even in the church. I ignored these signs and thought he'd change with time, but he never did. Rather, it got worse.

A year into our relationship, he rented an apartment for me and I had to stop working. He had proposed I go back to school but since I didn't plan to marry him or stay long in the relationship, I rejected it and asked to learn a skill instead.

I finally talked him into relocating his wife to stay with him, but it turned out to be a bad idea. It was one form of quarrel or the other between them everyday. He'd come to me complaining bitterly about her and I'd always advise him to go back and make peace with her.

At some point, he would get so upset with me not supporting him but rather supporting a woman who's supposed to be a threat to me. I couldn't even imagine what the woman was going through, I was just imagining me not living with him and was crying all night let alone someone living with him. It must have been hell for her.

Dating him was not as rosy as I thought. We had series of fights, he would insult me with every single thing I told him about myself. It has been one hell of a relationship, but I couldn't go back to where I came from. I didn't want to experience what I had experienced before I met him so I was stuck in the relationship.

In 2020, I got pregnant and I couldn't abort it. I told myself I should just marry him and rest, after all, he provides for me. That was how I gave him a child. He still didn't change but got worse by the day.

Last year, his wife finally left him. I wasn't happy about it because I couldn't handle the man all by myself. Though the wife had left at different times in the course of our relationship and even before I started dating him, this time, her leaving was permanent.

Her family was supportive so it was easy for her to leave. Let me also state that I wasn't the reason she left because his religion supports polygamy. As a matter of fact, I found out she's not the first wife of recent.

After she left, he insisted I move in with him which I did because there was no other option as he wouldn't pay my rent anymore and I had no savings.

Whenever he gave me money, he would ensure I used it for the last kobo. Moving in with him made me see through him. I realized there were other sides of him I had never seen and the relationship was my worst mistake.

I shouldn't have dated him in the first place, I shouldn't have let greed cloud my judgment. I was 20 and he was 34 when we met. I was suffering, yes,but I had freedom.

Right now, he has stopped me from visiting my only sister. He won't let me travel home. He even ordered me to always dress in wrapper and blouse whenever I'm going outI can't greet or talk to anyone and it looks like my life has ended."

PEACE

"I moved to Akwa ibom during my Nysc, I've been here since then. My life right now is a mess. The only hope I have is Jesus Christ.
I clocked 28 on January 12th, yet no serious relationship.

My body count is more than 15, but I only started having sex at 24. How did I get to this point? What is wrong with me? These are the questions I keep asking myself. I can't believe this . Not like I'm holy or the church type.

I used to be hard, but they broke my guard and I don't know who did. I had an abortion once and I've asked God to forgive me. I don't even feel the guilt any more because I believe my sins have been forgiven.

I am so weak. I wasn't like this, I don't know what is wrong with me. Not like the people I'm having sex with are asking me out or anything. They're just people I know and won't have anything to do with in the future. So why am I doing this? It's not like I'm taking money from them .

Before now, I didn't give in to sex no matter what.

I didn't mind struggling throughout the night if I spend the night in a guy's house. I wouldn't let him touch me.

But now, I can't help myself. Sometimes I cry and pray. I want to meet a strong man of God who can help me. I'd meet someone now and on the 2nd day, I'd be under him already .

I've always wanted to marry at 24. Suitors came early, but I wanted to get to 24 years of age. By then, I would have been done with school and service.

At 25, suitors came, but I was picky. I had them at 26 and 27 too, but I don't know what usually happens. I might just get irritated all of a sudden and cut all forms of communication.

Do I have spiritual problems? I've had different people tell me something about me being a child of water .

I don't know. I've had them tell me about reincarnation too and belonging to a secret cult. Something I don't even know about.

Right now I am struggling to collect my rent fee which expired in December, but the landlord gave me days of grace. Things are not going well at all. I need to see a strong man of God.

I feel my life is coming to an end. Sometimes I pray not to wake up.

Doing spiritual work costs money, I don't have the money. I've done it twice years back, with the help of my family, but they keep saying they didn't do it well.

I am tired. I need help. Now I don't know if I am pregnant. I'm scared to go for a test. I am patiently waiting for a missed period. My period is in 8 days. Only heaven will contain my joy if I see my period. I'm seeing early signs of pregnancy even though I had protected sex.

My life is a mess right now. I can't believe I'm living this kind of life. This isn't the life I worked hard for. Something is wrong somewhere. "

ADURA

"I have been married for seven years. My husband is a loving and caring man. He caters to all my needs even though I have a job.

After the first year of our marriage, I became pregnant and had a baby girl. I have tried to conceive since then to no avail. I discussed it with my husband so we could seek medical help, but he told me there was nothing wrong with me, and that I was being paranoid.

I was not satisfied with that response, so I decided to seek a solution on my own. I confided in a friend who advised me to see a spiritualist.

She took me to the man who told me that my husband was the reason for my inability to conceive.

He demanded 200,000 naira before he would commence treatment and cleansing. Right there, I transferred the money to him and he gave me some items to apply on my body.

All this while, I thought it was only my friend and I that knew about my mission, I didn't know that she had told my husband.

Few days after I visited the spiritualist, my husband confronted me with the issue, but I tried to deny it. He threatened to end our marriage if I didn't tell him the truth. I had no other option than to tell him everything.

I almost lost my marriage if not for the intervention of my family. I have learnt never to trust anybody. I have also stopped using the things I got for peace to reign. I'll be patient and wait for my next fruit to come at the right time."

HELEN

"When my sister wanted to remarry, I was completely against it. She already had four children from her previous marriage that ended badly. I told her to focus on raising them instead of seeking to marry another man, but she told me off.

I knew a bit about the man's background and I was certain he had nothing tangible to offer her. My sister was bent on marrying him so there was nothing much I could have done.

After two years of marriage, I noticed she was losing weight. I asked her what the problem was and she told me she was financially handicapped and had to do all kinds of menial jobs to sustain the family.

Apparently, her husband could not cater to their needs. When I reported her condition to other members of my family, they decided to step in and assist her. We pooled funds together and set up a business for her, but through poor management, it did not survive.

Recently, she became sick and was rushed to the hospital. After much diagnosis, it was confirmed that she had contracted the deadly virus.

When her husband heard the result, he ran away. Nobody knows where he is right now. It is obviously, he infected her with the virus.

My sister's health has declined. She is slipping away gradually. There's nothing much we can do but support her children. If only she had listened to me, she won't be where she is today. "

CYNTHIA

"I am a single mom of one. I became a single mom as a result of being jinxed/hypnotized. It's a long story for another day. I picked up my life and started taking care of my kid. I was able to save up some money then I decided to venture into selling thrifts at my workplace.

It went well the first time and I decided to go bigger. I set out to Sango from where I live to get the clothes one very early morning, got into a bus with about 4 men and two ladies with me making us 7. The others urged the driver to set out that he should pick people on the way.

I left home at 3:30 a.m because I needed to beat traffic and go to work that evening since I was on night shift. That was how we set out, I never knew I had entered "one chance."

The driver took a turn to somewhere that looked like a street and stopped. I don't know the route well so I never suspected anything. They asked me and one man to step down and submit our belongings, the street was bushy and lonely.

I had only 20k cash with me and they took it. They asked for my phone, but I refused to give it out because that's where my ATM card was. I didn't even know they were with a gun until that moment. One of them hit my left shoulder with the gun because I was struggling with one of the ladies for the phone. She later took it.

One of them said they would teach me a lesson for being too stubborn. These guys gang r#ped me. The only innocent person in the bus was the man they had beaten mercilessly for having nothing on him. I begged, I screamed, I asked for death that minute. I wished to even be in hell instead of that scene. I kept pleading till I had no strength.

The only thing in my head was "this cannot be happening to me again for the second time in a lifetime. God, you can't let me be gang r#£ped again in life."

Right there my life flashed before my eyes. I begged them to shoot me. The last one even spat on me and called me stubborn. Why won't I be stubborn? I had 191k in my account which was my life savings. I know I had my rent to pay come February and I have no helper anywhere.

Somehow I found my way home through some help I got. I only told my mom I was robbed because it would break her. I took myself to the hospital. These devils cleared my account and my sweats.

My shoulder still hurts like hell. I am sometimes hostile to my child especially anytime he wants to sleep on my arm. This is not who I am.

Few days ago, the landlord sent me a text to vacate the house. To think I worked so hard only to lose everything is killing me.

My baby daddy doesn't support me with anything. In fact, I don't have his contact. My mom went to a church yesterday, she hasn't been to the church before, it was her first time. The pastor told her to tell her first daughter to be wary of my baby daddy because he is doing everything possible spiritually to get me back to him.

Same yesterday, an unknown number called me and it turned out to be him. He asked meet up, that he knew I was having some challenges and he'd like to help.

I told him the only challenge I had was my house rent and I had paid it, (which is a lie) I could sense the shock. I ended the call and blocked the number.

I met someone here on FB who is offering to take me to Libya for a domestic job. I have heard stories about there but at this point, I am asking myself "what is the point of the good girl you have been trying to be all these while? " The pain in my shoulder on a daily basis reminds me of my ordeal. I have panic attacks."

ANDREW

My wife and I didn't date much, we only visited each other on a few occasions before we wedded. I discovered my wife didn't know how to cook.. her food was the type that could make anyone stay far away from home. I tried to manage it but damn, it wasn't manageable. I made up my mind to enroll her in a catering school around us..

It was one week after our wedding, we couldn't afford to pay a cook yet, we needed to plan properly. My phone rang and I walked slowly to go pick it up.

"Hey big bro. How's your new wife? Well, the whole family has planned to come have lunch at your place tomorrow, before they all return back to their respective places. So tell your wife to make us something real good," the sonorous voice of my younger sister Amaka came from the other end of the phone.

I nearly peed on myself, "when you say the whole family, who and who are coming?" I managed to ask her, beads of sweat dropping from my body even though the Ac was on.

"Hey bro, everyone, uncles, cousins, aunties, they will come for lunch ," my sister confirmed my fears.

How do I tell them that my wife doesn't know how to cook? Ha, of course I wouldn't like to embarrass my wife. What will she cook now? I myself can't cook but if I boil water eeeh... choi..

My wife's soup is nothing to talk about, her soup, water will be one side, meat will be another side.. Her stew is the definition of "okokobioko."

This one week, my stomach has seen "shege" but I was hoping to register her in the catering school before "banza" will enter.

I took out my phone to call the caterers. I had their contacts but they all said they were booked as it's the weekend. At this point I understood the difference between "finished" and "completely finished."

My wife came to the living room, she saw me sweating and asked what was wrong with me. I looked at her face, I loved her, I wanted to save her this life time embarrassment but I didn't know what to do. I just informed her of my sister's call, and she, like me, started sweating profusely,we both knew she would be tense.

"But baby what can I cook for them?" My wife asked with a shaky voice.

Fast forward to the next day, my wife and I woke up with a missed feeling. She couldn't sleep the whole night. She kept turning around. I gave her some money to buy something to make soup. She reluctantly collected the money.

After a few long hours..she finally came back. I asked her what she wanted to cook. She said she would make vegetable soup. I left her in the kitchen and went back to the room. The lunch was fixed for 12 noon. I checked the time it was already 11 am and my wife has been in the kitchen since 9am. I decided to go check up on her.

"Hey baby, is the food not ready ?" I opened the vegetable soup and as usual the soup wasn't souping at all. The vegetable was one corner while oil faced another side like a husband and wife that just had a fight.

My sister had already said that they were at the door, so I quickly went to usher them into the dining table after a few pleasantries.

"Hey baby. Just scoop the whole soup into a bowl and hand it over to me while you follow me with the eba. Make sure you put in the whole soup ." I instructed my wife.

I carried the whole soup in the bowel while my wife followed behind me with the eba.

I got to the dining table and intentionally hit my leg on the table, I fell down and poured the soup on the floor.

Everyone rushed to me, trying to help me get to my feet with a sounding "sorry, sorry. Hope you are not injured"

I cried bitterly, I refused to be consoled "did you injure yourself?" One of my aunts asked me how I was feeling, concerned.

"If I injure myself, it is not the problem. The problem is the soup I poured away. How will you people eat now?" I cried again. "Honey please go and get another soup" I said to my wife.

"Baby there's no more soup, remember you told me to scoop the whole soup,"

I started crying again and wailing, my family started consoling me. They even said I shouldn't worry about the soup, they offered to take me to the hospital but I declined. I went into the fridge to get a bottle of chin chin for them, they ate happily as we watched a movie while my wife trashed the soup.

After they left, I laughed out loud that my wife thought I had gone kolo. I told her what I did, I told her how I used my antics to save her the embarrassment and she joined me to laugh.

Today I'm eating a very delicious vegetable soup from my wife with smiles on my face. She has learned so well and her cooking now is heavenly.

ULOMA

I went to the market, after buying the things I needed, it was fine to go home. I boarded a bus, the bus was empty as it was still loading.

"Nne enter na," the driver said.

"No, I will wait make everybody to enter before I will enter," I replied.

Eh na, people of God, I'm one of the people that like to sit at edge, that place that conductor used to sit, yes because I want fresh air 😑 😑..

"Nne enter make others see chance na," the driver repeated and other passengers joined him.

"O na eme fine girl," (she's doing fine girl) one of the guys who urged me to stay inside while he sits there said.

I totally ignored them, even rolling my eyes in the process. When they noticed that they couldn't convince me to go inside they took their seats while I sat at the edge..

Come and see the triumphant smiles on my face, little did I know that I was dancing to the beating of surugede(Dance of the spirits).

Ala Owerri ndi nwenm Le e....it wasn't up to five seconds we entered the road, it started raining. I kept pretending as if I was well, when I couldn't take it anymore.

"Oga driver, this your door no dey close?" I asked out of anger.

"No vex fine girl the door no dey close o.. that's why I dey tell you make you enter inside that time," he said..

Eliza nwunem, o ka m si jee (is this how i suffer myself).. my village people has finally caught up with me.

I looked at the faces of other passengers, I know in their minds they will be like "ehe God don catch you."

Na so rain take finish me, upon say I die inside the bus, because I wan sit down for edge. These drivers can never make heaven.

WOFIA

"I was still in the university when my boyfriend proposed to me. He wanted us to get married immediately since he was planning to travel overseas, but I told him to give me some time to finish my studies.

He insisted on meeting my family to formalize our engagement. I accepted and a little introduction was carried out.

A few months later, he traveled. Then he started becoming obsessed with me. He would call several times a day. He even got his friend to spy on me. I wondered why he suddenly became paranoid.

Meanwhile, there were times I would call him and a lady would pick up. When I asked who she was, he told me she was his colleague. I was not satisfied with his response and decided to investigate. I found out he was living with another woman over there.

I confronted him over it, but he denied. When I kept pressing him to tell me the truth, he finally admitted but said we'd talk about it when he got home.

He came back after a year and wanted to hasten the marriage process. Each time I brought up the issue, he'd waive it aside. I had to stand my ground and insist on knowing before we can progress with marriage plans.

That was when he told me he had to move in with her to increase his job opportunities and also getting full residency. I have heard these stories before and I knew he wasn't telling the whole truth. It is possible he's already married to her.

I just couldn't continue with the marriage and told him so. I do not want to get into a relationship I do not understand and that might turn around to haunt me later. What was even more annoying was his constant policing when he was free to do as he pleased.

It was difficult breaking off the engagement considering how far we had come, but I'm glad I did. After all, they say a broken engagement is better than a broken marriage. "

LILLY

My guy and I were coming back from a function, he bashed someone's car. We both quickly came out to see the level of damage, thank God it wasn't serious, just a scratch.

The guy and his girlfriend came out from the car, while we were still apologizing the guy said it was "okay."

Omo the next thing, the girl started shouting, "what is okay, are you people blind, can't you see?" This girl talks plenty of things so, before you know it, she has removed her wig to fight.

My guy was giving me an eye to fight, or show her craze, but I ignored, and told him to come let's go. I don't know whether the girl escaped from the yaba. We got home and this guy asked me why I didn't fight the girl.

"Fight wetin? When Jesus has already fought all our battles."

This small relationship when I just entered, now dem don dey send me go battlefront.

Well i'm happy today.

CHIJIOKE

"I have incubated this pain for so long, it is time to ease myself.
I was sexually molested countless times.
When I was small, not up to 10 years old.
There is a place my mom used to drop us to play with other children.
There is one uncle there anytime mom drops me and leaves.
He will sexually abuse me and threaten me not to tell anyone or he will kill me.
This happened countless times more than 6 times.
Later I told my mom that I don't want to go to that place again.
She changed to another place for me.
That place she changed for me is the worst .
The uncle now will be abusing me everyday and he will give me 20# to buy nzu (white chalk) to lick .
With a threat that I should not tell my mom.
He abused me severally
Then I was in primary school.
Every time he sees me in my mom shop he will be calling me my wife.
My people will take it as a joke.
I have hated that guy till now.
I feel like hurting him.
Though he is married with children, I hate him.
He has begged me countless times to forgive him.
But the pain is still there.

ABUJIE

When I gained admission into the university, the plan was to live with my sister who was already in the university. A few weeks of my stay with her was met with so much disagreement and quarrel. For peace to reign, I decided to move out. I stayed with a friend for a month before I got my own accommodation.

I had a friend who was also stranded and in need of a place to stay. She pleaded for me to take her in for just a month which I accepted. After the third month of her stay with me, I realized she was not making any effort to get an accommodation. That was when I told her that if she planned to be with me, she would have to contribute to the rent when it was due for renewal, and she agreed.

When the time came for renewal and I informed her, she refused to contribute. I was angry with her and told her to leave my house if she would not bring the percentage we agreed on.

That night, we exchanged words and I angrily left the house to go sleep over at another friend's house.

I came back in the afternoon, the next day and shortly after I got home, the police came knocking on my door. I was arrested and taken to the station where I was informed of my crime.

I was told that I sent some boys to rape her and that was why I decided to go somewhere else to sleep. I spent two nights in the police cell before my family got a lawyer to handle the situation. I was denied bail at first as the Police said they'll be charging me to court.

I spent about a week in detention before we finally reached a settlement by paying the amount they asked for me to be released.

By the time I got back, she had moved out and for long, I didn't see her. I believe she deliberately avoided crossing paths.

To think that she would come up with such an allegation against me beats my imagination. Since then, I learnt my lesson and do not bring anyone into my house, definitely not females.

ROSE
"I need encouragement!

I am married with two kids,I got married to my husband as a virgin .. ever since I got married to this man, I have been supportive ,I am not a demanding wife, I don't wear trendy clothes like my mates,I carry dread locs just to make sure I don't demand ...but my husband wouldn't stop cheating on me ,he cheats on me with everything and it hurts because he does it to my face ...I have become a bitter person, I cry to sleep, wake up crying ...I feel If I die , my kids will suffer because my hubby will mistreat them...

Recently he started dating a married woman. The husband of the lady called me to warn my hubby. He locked him up in the police station, he slept at the police station for days ..but even when he was released, he taunted me that my prayers had come to pass that I connived with the lady's husband to lock him up . I cried. I have lost all my self-esteem. I don't go out, I can't stay in the midst of people.

I feel everyone is laughing at me , I can actually hear their voices in my ear . I could feel people mocking me.

I want to be left alone where no one will find me forever . I know I have lost my mind. I talk when walking on the street . I laugh on my own ..I have no money, this man has borrowed everything from me ..I have no friends, no family, and I'm alone in this world .. The family I know said I'm mad. I have been to a mental hospital before. I don't want to go back there. It's not a place to be . . ..I pretend I'm okay but deep down I want to wander around the street ..my antidepressants are not working anymore ..I want to run away but to where , I want to move out but I am trapped . ..

He mocks me in my vulnerable state , he snaps at me and sends it to this married lady ..I am tired when I am single. I was a devoted Christian who prayed to get it right because I have suffered from childhood ..I prayed, I fasted ,I didn't sleep around. I kept myself till marriage then why am I suffering. My kids are suffering, they no I am not okay but they can't help me they are 9 and 11 ...I am tired, I am tired .. If I end it, who will care for my kids? I am tired . I am tired . Life has beaten me."

JANET

"My younger sister took in a guy she met where she went to write her Waec exam last year. The boy is nowhere to be found.

My sister doesn't even know where he stays or where he's from and she doesn't know the name he's answering in school.

I searched for the guy the best way I could but my efforts were in futility. I decided to let her join me here in Lagos because I couldn't take her to the village to go stay with our mother.

My Mom developed HBP ever since we lost our father last 2 years and staying with her might worsen her condition. I don't want to lose her.

She joined me here in Lagos. I used the little money I had saved to rent a room for us because before now, I was sleeping in a shop where I was working at a restaurant in Festac.

She cries every night and day. I try my best to make sure she's okay. They pay me 1k daily where I work. My problem now is that recently, she called me and thanked me for all I have been doing for her.

She added that she's tired of this life. She said that after giving birth in a few months time, she would leave the baby with me and travel to Georgia.

I asked her what she's going there to do and with who? She said that she's going there to do surrogacy and get paid. That they promised to pay her 7 million and many other benefits including allowances.

I have tried talking sense into her, but she keeps saying that nothing will stop her from going.

Please I need advice on what to do and how to handle this. I have searched for a job for her to be working, but there's no work anywhere.

We are really suffering, but I can't stand to see her go this way before she will end up in the hands of a ritualist. I really need advice and wisdom to handle this. I am 27 years old while she's 24.

She said that her flight, visa and accommodation fees are on her sponsor.

I have tried getting the number of the person she's making this arrangement with, but her phone has fingerprint protection and passwords."

MARGRET

"If someone had told me I'd be alive today, I would have doubted it. There were many times I gave up. There were times the medical team also gave up.

My family got tired. I cannot even begin to explain how tough it was for my children. They were without a father and their mother was hospitalized for months with no hope of coming out alive.

It was in 2019 I was diagnosed with ovarian cancer. I went through several phases of chemotherapy. I was in a coma for over two months as a result of the chemotherapy.

When I came out of the coma, other complications started. I became paralyzed. I was so emaciated you could see through my skin to my bones. I developed an ulcer. Of course, my hair was gone.

In addition to all the physical pain, there was also the mental torture. After the first time my children came to see me and broke down crying, I couldn't let them go through it again.I stopped them from seeing me. Imagine having to go months without your children, when they were all you've got.

I sold everything. I lost my business because those I left it with couldn't manage it in my absence. My husband's family supported the kids, while my own family supported with some bills and taking care of me at the hospital.

I guess that helped because if not for the support, I would have died even from thinking alone. My recovery was slow, but I am here now.

My hair has grown back. I have a job and am saving towards starting my business again. My children are doing fine. I look back at that year and where I am now and I know it's just God's grace that kept me."

JANET

"I can't remember exactly what caused our quarrel. I had moved out of the house I shared with my sister some months back just so we could have our peace since we could not stay together in peace.

One day, a family friend called to talk to me about reconciling with my sister. He insisted I move back to the house. I accepted just so he wouldn't keep talking about it but had no plans to go back to the house even if I were to reconcile with her.

Then one evening, I had just returned from work when I had this strong urge to see her. I pushed it aside and prepared to settle in for the night, but the thought of seeing her wouldn't leave my mind.

When I could no longer ignore it, I decided to go. I got to the house and let myself in since I still had a key. I was shocked when I found my sister convulsing on the floor. I screamed for help, ran out to call her neighbor and together we were able to take her to the hospital.

The diagnosis was cerebral malaria and the doctor said if not for my timely intervention, she would have gone into a stroke or had a cardiac arrest.

We ended up spending about a week in the hospital and when she was discharged, I didn't need anyone to tell me to go back home. I can't help but wonder what would have happened if I had held on to my anger or not obeyed my instincts that night. I wouldn't have forgiven myself. "

MR&MRS OLU

"Growing up, I heard it said many times that my tribe was forbidden to marry from theirs. There is a story around it, but I never paid much attention to let it sink in. I just knew that people from that tribe were off limits.

We met in the university far away from home. It was love at first sight for us and we kicked off immediately. Though I found out his tribe soon enough, I had forgotten about the prohibition and it never crossed my mind.

On his part, he had not heard of it then and so there was no way he could have brought it up. Because we were far away from home, our families didn't get to know about the relationship.

We had dated for over a year when I finally told my elder sister about him. It was she who reminded me of the tradition and told me to break ties with him immediately.

When I told him about it, he laughed and dismissed it saying we shouldn't be following such traditions in modern times, especially since I couldn't tell him the story behind it. That emboldened me and I told my sister I was not going to break up with him.

That was how it got to my parents and I was summoned. They advised, threatened and said things that made me scared, but I was deeply in love and couldn't bring myself to end the relationship.

When we asked his parents, they admitted knowing about the tradition but do not adhere to such things. That so long as we were good with each other, they'd give their blessings.

We continued dating and a year later, started planning our marriage. When it was obvious my parents won't accept the marriage, his own parents advised us to reconsider our stance and go our separate ways rather than lose my family's blessings and relationship.

My husband is a very stubborn person and he outrightly refused. Seeing the way he stood up for me, I had to join him in our resolve. That strained my relationship with my family and his too.

In the course of all these, I got pregnant and we decided to keep it. He was doing well and so could take care of me. I moved in with him. My mum and sister could no longer let me go through that pregnancy alone so they reconnected with me.

My dad was the only one who refused to have anything to do with me. He practically chased my husband out of the house the day he went to plead with him. My child was 6 months before he saw us and another year before he agreed to the marriage.

It's been over ten years now with three kids. Nothing of the things they said has happened. We have our issues, but our marriage is a good one. I am glad my husband stood his ground and I stood with him and not let fear stand in the way of our love."

GIFT

"I'm a married woman, but there is something that keeps bothering me. Since I got married, I have not had any peace of mind.

When I was still single, I was dating two people.

One is my current husband . When we were still dating, I had my eyes on one man. I just wanted to play along to be honest. Please don't judge me, I know I messed up.

We finally started dating. I kept falling in love with him and I couldn't go a day without thinking of him. He spent a lot of money on me. I told him I had a fiancé, but he begged me not to leave.

To cut the story short, I later got married and we broke up. Because I promised myself never to have any affair when I get married, I stayed away from him.

However, since I got married I have not had any rest of mind. I have gone for confession and asked God for forgiveness. I have also asked my ex for forgiveness, but, still I have not had any peace of mind. I keep having issues with my husband everyday. Anytime I sleep, I see my ex in my dream almost every night. I don't know what to do. "

HENRY

"I knew her through a married friend. They were dating then. We all knew nothing was going to come out of the relationship, it was just for them to have fun and move on when they get tired of each other.

At the same time, another friend was showing interest in her without any objection from the friend she was dating. In fact, that friend gave us the go ahead to have our share of her if we wanted.

It turned out she didn't like the second friend but rather started showing interest in me. She would call to check up on me and was just showing extra care.

I began to get drawn to her and in no time became intimate. That was my first mistake. No matter what my friend had said, I shouldn't have gotten involved with her. But rather than go my way and let them continue their affair, I started an affair with her.

Before long, she told me she was pregnant. By now, she had ended the affair with my friend. We decided to keep the baby.

At this point, I still had not taken her as a serious girlfriend. As her pregnancy progressed, she proposed she move into my house and I agreed. That was another mistake on my part and that was how we became live -in partners for over four years.

Because she now has my child and has been living with me as a wife, I treated her right. I was doing quite well then so money wasn't the problem.

What worried me was her unseriousness with life. She wouldn't complete her education. I gave her money at different times to start businesses, but it always flopped after a short while. She preferred to party with friends and go shopping.

The worst part was that her family could not talk to her. I had met them at this point and they were also mounting pressure on me to come marry her properly. I honestly wanted to but each time I got ready, she would do something so annoying that'd make me change my mind.

That was how we went on till the Covid period when my business was no longer functional and the money dwindled.

She became abusive and even violent. She abandoned the child to the maid. She would nag morning and night especially over marrying her. That was when I came to the realization that I had made a mistake and decided I will never marry her.

It also dawned on me that she would never change because even while she was under my roof, she was still taking money from male friends but denies having anything to do with them.

I started having doubts about the paternity of my son and though I have been advised to go do a DNA test, I cannot bring myself to do it.

I don't know if it's because the money was no longer coming or that she realized I won't marry her that she decided to leave. But to punish me, she left when I wasn't around and without any information on where she was going with the aim of denying me access to my son.

It took a lot of trouble with her family before she eventually surfaced. It got to the point that we had to go to welfare services to reach an agreement on the custody of and access to our child.

When I think back, I wonder if I was with my senses then. How I would think that I could actually build something meaningful with someone like that. I had some terrible years with her, but I'm glad to finally be free. So long as I can see my son as agreed and still be a part of his life, I am fine. "

GOODNESS
Part 1

"When a man tells you it's just sex he wants, my sister run for your life because even if you kill yourself,it will still be just the sex for him.

So I met this guy on my birthday when I went to the hospital to visit my uncle. He is a medical doctor—young, fresh, fine, black guy. Exactly my spec.

For me, it was LOVE AT FIRST Sight. immediately I saw this guy. I liked him and wished he would come ask me out, but he did not even notice my presence and based on the fact that I'm an African woman I couldn't approach him.

I looked at his name and quietly typed it in my phone. (I created a WhatsApp for me where I write about some of my issues. It's like a Diary)

After I wrote his name down, I prayed quietly within myself that if it was God's will, we should meet again and let him ask me out.

Few days passed and luckily for me, I was scrolling through Facebook and saw him on my friend's suggestions. I said to myself, "this is the Lord's doing." I sent him a friend request. He accepted immediately and I was very happy within me, not knowing I was digging my own grave.

I sent him a "hi", he responded. We started chatting and from there we moved to WhatsApp. I don't know how it happened, but we moved pretty fast and then after 2 months of being together, I noticed he wasn't into the relationship as I thought it'd be.

I decided to get things defined. He opened up to me that he didn't want to be committed to the relationship because he had a girlfriend and she's abroad. He said we should just be having fun and that he was not even on speaking terms with his girlfriend.

Instead of walking away, I stayed put. The truth is, I was already neck deep in love with him. I felt since they were not on talking terms and if I showed him how much I genuinely love him, things might be well with us.

That was where my problem started. I was still struggling in school,but I'd take the little money I had to make soup for him, buy him gifts and do other things. I practically worshiped the ground he walked on. I would also watch porn to improve my sex skills.

Gradually things became so good between us. He was a weed smoker and was addicted to cigarettes. He taught me how to smoke weed. We'd puff weed and have sex all night. The sex was just too good. All my Life, I had never had such pleasure before (I'm 28yrs he is 33).

It continued till I got pregnant for him. I told him about it and he said I should remove it, that we weren't ready for a child. I tried to convince him, but he refused based on the fact that I was still schooling. I accepted and had my first abortion. "

Part 2

"Then I noticed I was the one always calling, texting, and gifting, for the 4yrs we were together. He never for once gave me a single gift. Throughout the 4yrs of the situationship, he didn't call me up to 3 times and I wasn't bothered.

The only thing in my head was just to prove myself to him that I genuinely loved him and not after material gains. I so wanted him that I was willing to do just anything for him.

After a while I was no longer satisfied with the fact that he could go for weeks without calling me until I called.

Sometimes I'd call him for 3 days straight, he'd not pick nor return my calls or texts. He'd always claim he was busy. He even went ahead to say that I call him too much, that I should minimize the way I call him.

This whole thing continued gradually and I noticed he was always broke. Sometimes he'd collect money from me for weed—amount as little as 2k. I'd always give him. I even sent him a recharge card. He is from a middle class family. His parents are doing well, so he doesn't have any responsibilities at home, yet he was always broke.

I started complaining about his attitude towards me. He'd always tell me we were just sex partners and nothing more. Instead of me moving on with my life, I'd still stay put. The more I stayed, the better the sex and it became more intense. The chemistry between us also improved.

He'd receive an award at work, I'd be the one to write citations for him, speeches etc. I knew everything about him. Whenever we were together, we'd be in each other's arms wrapped in love but the moment I left, he'd become so cold and distant.

I got so addicted to him that I couldn't go a day without hearing his voice. We discussed everything. He'd tell me about his job and successful surgeries he had carried out. I could feel the love in his heartbeat and voice when he talked to me.

Yet each time I asked him to be committed to me, he'd tell me it's just sex we were having, he had a girlfriend, yet I still stayed, I stayed supporting him and encouraging him that things would get better.

He was so broke that I was wondering how a medical doctor could be so broke just 1 week after collecting salary not knowing he had been paying flight tickets to and fro at intervals for his foreign main babe to visit and I didn't know. All this continued, but I still stayed till I had a second abortion.

I called him one day after trying to reach him for 3 days. A lady answered and said she was his girlfriend and that I should stop calling her boyfriend. He said he didn't want to talk to me.

Since I'm not a troublesome person, I ended the call.

Few minutes later, he called me and said he was sorry for the way his babe talked to me. That he left his phone to charge and was at work when she answered me. He said he forgot to mention to me that his babe was around, so I wouldn't be calling. Afterwards, he blocked me.

I cried my eyes out that day and decided to end things. I stayed without reaching him for 1 week and it felt like I was going to run mad. Then I discovered I was pregnant for the 3rd time. "

Part 3

"I called him with another line, he asked me to get rid of it and I did. Mind you, he never gave me any money! I financed all the abortions I had. He blocked me from calling him and said it was because I was calling him a lot, but he didn't block me on WhatsApp so we were still communicating on WhatsApp. We were sending each other nudes.

His babe left. I begged him to unblock me. He did and we continued from where we stopped. I was so confused. I'd go on Google looking for answers about our relationship (a Virgo male and a Capricorn female relationship). Google described the relationship as "a match made in heaven". Yet he kept blocking and unblocking me at intervals.

My mum is late. I'm the first daughter in my family. I am a core introvert. I don't go out or have friends. I never had anyone to advise me or correct me. My head was filled with him and just him. My mental health was destroyed.

We had sex again last December and this January, I discovered I was pregnant again. I told him I was going to keep the baby whether he liked it or not. He said it was not his concern since decided to be a single mother.

When he knew I was serious about my decisions, he opened up to me that his girlfriend had been around since the 4 months he stayed away from me. He said she was heavily pregnant and currently staying in his family house.

That they were engaged and planning to get married as soon as she put to bed.

He was coming to have sex with me while he had his pregnant girlfriend at home. After he told me this, it's like scales fell off my eyes. I asked him what happened all these four years we were together. He didn't even feel remorseful. He said he told me we were just sex partners from the onset. He said he blocked me several times for my own good, yet I ignored his warnings.

He said he loved his girlfriend and she even loved him more than I think I love him and that I shouldn't make him feel guilty for cheating on her.

I then asked him for money to do the abortion,but he still didn't have any. I struggled and used my money to do it. This time after doing it, I fainted at the hospital. immediately I came back, I quietly blocked him on Facebook and everywhere.

Till today I wake up everyday crying to God, asking why he allowed me to do this kind of wickedness to myself? I can't tell if it was the weed, sincerely I can't tell what happened to me.I'm just begging God for his forgiveness. I think I need therapy. If not, I might just wake up dead one day."

Part 4

"I'm healed and I have moved on. I'm only sharing this story right now because I want people to learn from my mistake.

For some, I know I caused all this pain for myself, but you wouldn't entirely blame me for staying this long. I saw mixed signals that made me hope for more. Sometimes when we were together, he'd tell me, "you worry too much, stop thinking about the future. We will be alright. "

Sometimes when his abroad girlfriend would video call him, he wouldn't answer, he'd grumble and reject the call. It all seemed like he was confused and needed time to end his relationship.

He told me he was having issues with her because of me. He made me understand that he was already committed before we met and I should keep giving him time to end things with her.

Some people assumed I'd still accept him if he came back. But the truth is, I wouldn't. He will marry his girlfriend as soon as she gives birth and they will leave the country together.

In his own words: "this is life, we all made our choices, we won't work and we will never work for reasons best known to me. Get rid of the pregnancy and move on."

He wouldn't dare reach out to me ever again, not in this life. We had a deep sexual chemistry. If it seems too good for you to believe, read about a Virgo male and a Capricorn female sexual connection you will understand more.

We also had deep intellectual discussions. He told me I was very intelligent. That if I should let myself out to the world a little bit, I'd be noticed. All of this was a big boost to my self esteem.

He played chess and was a very smart guy. He just used my vulnerability to get me tied down. My only mistake was that I had the chance to walk away, but I didn't. I have now realized my worth. I didn't keep the last pregnancy because that'd be a link he could use to come back to me.

I made a mistake and I don't want to continue living with the stigma. I had a safe abortion and I'm good. I will still have babies in the future. Don't judge me.

God loves me so much. I used to wonder if being with him was really what I wanted. I thought about how to raise children together with his addictions (gambling and smoking). I reasoned all of the negative sides, but I just wanted to prove that people can still be loved genuinely with their imperfections.

I felt that with me by his side, he'd change. I just pray never to fall in love with the wrong person. My simple prayer to God right now is, "if he isn't the one for me, no matter how I feel Lord, let it not work. "

God saved me. I just dodged a bullet. At least now I wouldn't think about killing myself for a married man. My senses are back. I'm not addicted to weed. I don't drink alcohol. It's even easier for me to move on than I thought I would. Let him go in peace.

What is to come will always be better. Even if I meet him anywhere in life again, I'll laugh and pass like nothing happened. I have forgiven myself. If God is kind to me and give me another man, I'll still love again, but this time I'm fully equipped with all the knowledge I need."

OKENNA

"When I met my wife, she was not working and had no skills. After our wedding, I asked her what skill she would like to acquire and she opted for fashion and design. I paid for her registration and also bought a sewing machine to enable her practice at home.

After two years of learning, she could not master the art. I decided to open a provision store for her, but still, she could not break even. Instead, my wife was spending so much time attending all her church prayer meetings and other church programmes.

It was not long before the neighbors started talking. Some told me to keep an eye on her, that they suspected my wife was having an affair with her pastor. I didn't believe them because I felt they were rumor mongers.

One day, I traveled to the village to oversee my building project. I asked my wife if she would go with me but she declined.

When I got to the village, I told my wife to send the money I gave her to keep, but she told me she had given it to her pastor. I was very angry and had to return home the next day without informing her.

I got home to meet my wife with her so-called pastor in our bedroom. She was not properly dressed though he still had his clothes on. She claimed he came to pray for her.

Though I didn't catch them in an intimate position, it was very likely that was to happen and it may not be her first time. I have since sent her home to her family.

They've been calling me for a meeting, but I have refused to honor any. I'm still very angry so for now, it's best we both stay apart. "

DELIGHT

"I have been married for 5 years. When I was pregnant with our first baby, my husband advised me to go and stay with my mother since it's my first baby, so that she'd take care of me. I agreed with him.

I went to stay with my mum. Right from the first month till the ninth month, my husband refused to come check up on me. No visit. I was the one always calling him. He'd talk to me briefly and drop the call.

When I put to bed, my mum and siblings called him several times to come and bail me from the hospital, but he kept telling different stories till I stayed in the hospital for 1 week without any reason.

I gave birth freely without complications. The hospital asked us to leave so that they could have space on the bed, since my baby and I were okay.

My mum and siblings started calling my husband again, but it was the same story till my mum and siblings paid the hospital bill. I called him to say we were out of the hospital. He asked me to stay with my mum to do omugwo there. I stayed back.

After three months of the omugwo, I complained that I was tired of staying there and wanted to come back.

I went back to our house where my husband and I live. I asked him what happened that made him not visit us or even came to bail me from the hospital. He told me to forget about that since everything had been sorted out.

Fast forward to when I got pregnant with my second baby, he did exactly the same thing. My siblings almost got angry.

Now I'm pregnant with my third child and he's been ringing it in my ear to go to my mum's house. My siblings said I shouldn't come to inconvenience my mum because each time I come, she spends money taking care of me. And

it's my siblings that send money for upkeep for my mother.

My siblings will call him for an explanation, he won't say anything tangible. I will ask him, he will shut me up. If my siblings come to speak to him face to face in our house, he will leave the house. I don't know what's wrong. I'm tired.

He has refused to say what his problem is. Just acting as though he isn't doing anything wrong. If I try to talk to him, he will leave the house and not come back for a week or more.

Now my siblings have warned me seriously not to come back to the house to disturb my mother. That I should stay there and let him take responsibility. He has left the house because of that and refused to come for four days now.

I have called his siblings to complain. They all said he's an adult and they can't control or force him to do the right thing.

MARIAM

"I have been married to my husband for ten years. We have a daughter.

After our first child, I have not been able to conceive again. Before now, my husband never saw anything wrong with having only one child.

When his younger brother got married, and within a short time had three children, it became a big problem.

My husband would complain and grumble that it was not proper for his brother to have more children than him. I told him that instead of complaining and comparing himself to his brother, we should be thankful for the one we have.

One day, he told me he was going to get another wife. He insisted I relocate to the village, but I told him I was not going anywhere.

When I complained to his mother, she told me to allow her son to marry a second wife because she wanted more grandchildren. At this point, I knew I was alone since he had the support of his mother.

Last year, he traveled home and got himself a second wife. I have decided to focus on my daughter and my business and let him do whatever he wants. "

DESTINY

"We had been friends for sometime but because I was in a relationship then, we couldn't date though he had indicated interest.

After that relationship ended, he resumed his wooing. By this time, he had left the country. I decided to give him a chance.

I thought since we had been friends for a long time, a relationship should come easy. At the beginning, it was good. Though our time zones were different, we found time to communicate regularly.

In that time, he visited once and over time, I told my family about him and he also introduced me to him.

As the relationship progressed, he started talking of marriage. He planned to come home so we could put some plans into action but eventually couldn't because of some work obligations.

He then proposed that I come over instead. I was excited as it would be my first time travelling out of the country and it also proved to me his seriousness.

He started the arrangement and before long, I was on my way to see him.

I arrived there excited about the time we would spend together after over a year of not seeing each other.

The first week after I arrived was good. He took me places and when we were home, we had a nice time together.

By the following week, I was left alone. He would go off for days only to return without any explanation. He won't even call to let me know he won't be coming back home.

He would rather leave me with enough cash and ask me to go out, see places, go shopping.

Weeks turned into months like this and I became lonely and bored. He didn't even bring up the reason for my coming in the first place.

Anytime I mentioned it to him, he would dismiss me and call it nagging. He started saying I should be grateful for what I had and stop complaining as many ladies would gladly take my place.

After eight months, I couldn't take it anymore. I was gradually slipping into depression. I couldn't get a job, I couldn't do anything at all. The worst was that he was not even around to keep me company. His excuse was always work.

I had to ask myself if this was what I wanted in marriage. To have an absent husband that will never have time for family, that is if he eventually marries me. My answer was negative so I decided to return home.

He tried to delay it at first, but when it was obvious I was serious, he bought my ticket back.

After I returned, I tried to keep up with the relationship, but I was no longer feeling it and rather than keep holding us back, I ended it.

It's been over a year and sometimes I think I made a mistake and should have endured.

Other times, I am happy I left because I know I would have been unhappy still staying there. "

VICTOR

"When we were planning our wedding, my wife wanted a simple ceremony, which was fine with me since we would not be spending so much money.

Her mother, on the other hand, wanted something elaborate. Her reason was that she wanted everybody to know that her daughter was getting married.

Before now, there have been speculations that my wife's mother is a witch. Some of her siblings also believed it and that she's the one hindering them from progressing in life. I always thought it was ridiculous of them.

When my wife had her baby, her mum came to visit and was to go back the same day. She came with cooked food. As she presented the food to my wife, she said, " I know you people think that I'm a witch. If you don't want to eat the food you can throw it away."

After she left, I asked my wife if she would eat the food, and she said she would eat it.

Two weeks later, she started complaining of body aches. I thought it was due to stress. I bought her some drugs to relieve her of the aches. She felt better after a few days.

One night, we were getting ready to go to bed when she slumped and started convulsing. I rushed her to the hospital, but she was pronounced dead on arrival.

When I called her family to inform them of what had happened, they blamed their mother for her death.

I have made plans to bury her, but her siblings said they would like to investigate the cause of her death.

I do not know what to believe anymore. I wish they would allow me to bury her in peace because I don't want to imagine what their investigation can possibly bring out. Besides, she's gone and nothing we do will bring her back."

EBIERE

"I was sick seven years ago. I thought I was going to die. I was bedridden and couldn't walk.

Several tests were conducted, but it was difficult to ascertain the cause of my illness.

During that time some of my friends told me to seek an alternative since no diagnosis was made. One of them said my sickness was not ordinary, that it was an attack from my colleagues.

As much as I was desperate for healing, I was not ready to waste my money on unreliable sources. So, I told them that I would not seek an alternative. I believed that God would heal me through the doctors. There's a reason for the knowledge he gave to them.

A few days later, the diagnosis was made and I was given appropriate treatment. Even though it took me a while to heal, I'm happy I decided to remain in the hospital.

Some of my friends no longer talk to me because I refused to heed their advice, but I'm not bothered. I do not know if they were planning to scam me.

God is not confined to a room. You can pray to God wherever you are while receiving treatment from professionals."

LOVELYN

"When I read stories online about men blackmailing women over nude pictures, I never thought it would get to me.

I was not doing it with anyone. A few times I had been asked to send, I refused because I wanted to be on the safe side.

When I got married, my husband and I had a good sexual relationship. We had other issues, but sex was not part of the problem for us. In fact, we used it to settle most of our quarrels.

Shortly after our marriage, he got a job that took him offshores for months. Our sex life was affected because he was hardly home. It was difficult for me, but I was determined to be faithful in my marriage.

I also believed he was faithful, although I sometimes heard rumors of the kind of things they do on those sites.

When he suggested we should start sharing sex videos, I objected at first but he started using it to guilt trip me. I became worried that he might go seek for pleasure elsewhere if I didn't do as he said.

That was how we started. I'd make videos of myself and send them to him. I also became very protective of my phone.

Somehow, our petty quarrels degenerated to bigger ones. When he returned home finally, the quarrels just got worse and even became violent at times. That was when I started considering divorce.

When I told him my intentions, this man threatened to leak my videos to social media. He even went further to tell our pastor and our families that I was cheating on him while he was away and even sending nudes to men. He sent them some of the videos.

I really do not know what he was thinking because our chats were there. Maybe he thought I would be too ashamed or afraid to tell people the truth. I wasn't going to sit back and let him tarnish my image so I told everyone what actually happened.

In the long run, he abandoned me and my children and left the marriage. I only found out later from his employer that he had resigned and even traveled abroad.

Even his family was cut off. I was badly hurt and embarrassed by the whole situation, but I had to be strong for my children.

Now I tell ladies, even if the person is your husband, you have to be very careful because someone who you think you know today can turn into a totally different person tomorrow. "

JOSHUA

"I got married to my wife six years ago and since then, it's been from one trouble to another.

Before my marriage, I was working in a good company. Two weeks after our wedding, I got sacked without a good reason.

I felt it was one of those things of life and that I would get another job because it's not always hard for me to get a job.

But each company I went to in search of a job wouldn't want to employ me. That's where my troubles started as I had used part of my savings to run the marriage rites and wedding expenses.

My wife also got out of job because she became pregnant and was always falling sick. After spending so much in hospital bills, she would still lose the pregnancy—not once but six times.

I have even sold the land I managed to buy. We practically feed from hand to mouth and from friends.

I have gone for prayers in different places and they all said that my wife has a spirit husband that's causing the misfortunes. I have fasted, prayed, yet no solution.

Last week my brother called me and said he went the traditional way to find out what was happening to me, and the man said that my wife has a spirit husband.

I don't believe in traditional things but the pastors have also told me this previously.

My brother said that I have two options according to the man: Either to leave my wife or bring her to settle the spirit husband.

I'm so tired, I don't know what to do. I love my wife so much and I don't want to hurt her feelings. "

KENNETH

"I was outside my gate one evening when I heard noise and shootings. People started running. Before I knew what was happening, a Police van stopped in front of me. They were shouting,

" Hey, stop there. If you move,I shoot."

I became frozen in fear, stood there, and raised my head up. They came down from the Toyota hilux. They were four in number. Two held me so tightly and pushed me into the hilux.

I kept asking them what I did, but they told me to shut up and keep quiet, else they would shoot me.

I guess they were chasing someone and thought I was the person. I tried everything possible, but they still took me to the station after slapping me several times.

I was locked up. I couldn't even reach my wife and kids. I kept begging them to at least let me speak to my wife so that they would be aware of my whereabouts, but the police refused. They kept saying I was a criminal.

I cried my eyes out, I cried like a baby.

I stayed in the police custody for five days. On the fifth day, some people came to visit those in the cell. One of them asked me what my crime was. I told him that I did nothing with tears rolling down my eyes.

He was touched, he went to speak to the policemen and after a few minutes, I was brought out.

He paid for my bail and I was released. I kept thanking him. He gave me transport fare to go back home.

I went home shirtless because I wasn't wearing any clothes that day. I went home and met my wife and kids crying. I really thank God for saving me."

OLIVER

"When I married my wife, life was good. We had a comfortable life. Two years after the marriage, I lost my job, but I was still able to provide for my family.

My wife who was pregnant then was not happy. She told me this was not the life she bargained for. I did everything to make her comfortable because of her condition. I pleaded with her to give me time to look for a better job as I was not going to settle for anything less.

She told me she would leave after she had our baby, but I didn't think she was serious. Eight months after she delivered, while I was away from home, she abandoned our baby and took off.

It was a neighbor who called to inform me of the situation. When I got home, my baby was alone. I was heartbroken. I called her, but she told me she was not coming back and that I should look for someone who'd take care of the baby.

I had to get a nanny because my family members were far away.

It's been a year since my wife left us without looking back. My baby is doing very well and I have been restored.

My wife was only there for the money, not because she loved me.

I've not given up on love yet. I just want to take care of my child and develop myself as well. "

JOHN

"After my National Diploma from Abubakar Tatari Ali Polytechnic Bauchi in Dec 2014. I returned back to my base in Kaduna. I was also preparing to travel home for Christmas that year.

I called my beloved sister in Abuja to inform her about my journey and she told me to come early to spend some days with her before proceeding to the village for Christmas which I agreed to.

I spent some days with her in Abuja before I traveled home. When I came back, I still went to her house to say hi and to deliver a message from the village.

I wanted to go back to Kaduna the following day, but she stopped me to spend some days with her. While I was waiting, she discussed with her husband that I should stay with them in their house, since I was already through with school.

Also because they didn't have any male adults in their house that would be running errands for them like switching on the generator.

I wasn't that happy with the idea because I'm a guy. I needed to go and hustle on my own without depending on anybody, but I later agreed.

Fortunately for me, after some months, my sister's husband assisted me to get admission directly into the university. I was so happy.

I finished my school and my youth service successfully.

But something bad happened—my beloved sister fell sick and just a month after my passing out, the unexpected happened on my way coming from Katsina where I was serving.

I received a call thinking that it was just a normal call, but the call was for the death of my sister. It was just like a dream because I couldn't believe what I heard on the phone .

On reaching the hospital, the bed was empty. I asked the people where my sister was but no one answered me. I cried and cried , but my cry could not bring her back to life.

My life became shattered and unbearable. Everything changed and all hope was lost. June 6th 2019 remains an unforgettable day in my life. That was the day she departed from this wicked world.

The same year my sister died, her husband remarried. He got married to my niece. I didn't like the Idea of him marrying my family again ,but he said it's because of the children. He didn't want them to feel their mother's absence, that's why he decided to marry from my family.

When he finally married her, she packed into his house and everything turned upside down. She came with a bad attitude and nothing we did in the house pleased her.

In December 2021, she asked her husband to send me out of his house. My own niece. I didn't expect that from her and the husband agreed that I should go. A man I had been staying with for 5 years.I asked a friend to allow me move in with him. I'm going through a lot.

I have been searching for jobs here in Abuja all to no avail. I have gone to different interviews but no positive outcome. I do go out to sites for daily pay and I don't have enough money to learn a skill. I'm just here till God sends my destiny helper to locate me. "

REJOICE

"Two years ago, I relocated from my state to another state in search of greener pastures. A few months after my arrival, I got a teaching job at a private school.

I was doing my job diligently until one fateful day the head of the infant school summoned me to her office. She openly told me that I was a threat to her and I should be careful otherwise, I would be sacked.

I asked her if I had offended her, but she told me to leave her office. At that moment, I just had to apologize for peace to reign.

I left feeling disturbed. I decided to confide in a colleague who then told me the reason for the lady's annoyance with me. According to her, the infant head said I acted as if I knew it all, and that I was always minding my business. How is that a problem?

Sometime later, the directors of the school decided to restructure. They asked her to write down the names of people that should be sacked. My name was top of the list.

The day they asked us to leave the school premises, I was shocked to find her amongst us.

I have gotten a better job now and I'm happy. I pray she is happy too wherever she is, since I'm no longer a threat. I honestly do not know what some people stand to gain by being wicked."

ANGELA

"When my aunty got married, there was a little fracas on the wedding day between her and some of our family members.

Because of the incident, she decided to cut us off. We were left in the dark, unaware of how she was faring.

Some of my family members tried to reach out to her to no avail. We only got information about her from her friends. From what we heard, she was going through a lot in the marriage, coupled with the fact that she could not conceive. Her husband was abusing and cheating on her constantly. He finally left her for another woman.

After a while, she decided to adopt two children and was doing very well. Even with all her marital problems, she still didn't want to have anything to do with us. You can't force yourself on someone who doesn't want you so we left her alone.

A few months ago, she went to work and came back as usual with no sign of sickness. After she had dinner, she slumped and died. Now, the family that she rejected is running helter-skelter, making plans for her burial. The husband isn't contributing much.

I believe her husband capitalized on the fact that she was not in good terms with her family and decided to maltreat her. We also feel guilty that we didn't put in more effort. For me, I've learnt never to throw my family away because you never know when you might need them."

CONFIDENCE

When I graduated from secondary school, I had no intention of going to university because I had no one to train me.

My parents did not have the resources, so I resolved to do menial jobs to meet my needs and also assist my parents.

I have a friend who is overseas. One day she called and we had a lengthy conversation since we had not spoken for a long time. She inquired about my situation and how I was surviving. I told her everything, but she was not happy with the fact that I was not in school. She told me to start making plans to go back to school as she would support me financially. I was elated.

I told my parents and they were happy too. I wrote JAMB and was able to secure an admission. My friend has been paying for my school fees with little support from my parents.

I am now in my final year and she's already making plans for me to join her after graduation.

I am happy to have her in my life. If it wasn't for her I wouldn't be where I am today.

JACK

"My parents died when I was six years old. They had contracted a terminal illness that took their lives.

From the story I heard, they were stigmatized by both families. My dad had a bosom friend who was there for him throughout his trying times.

Before my dad died, he told his friend to adopt me as his child since his family was no longer interested in him and his family.

My father's friend took me in and has been taking care of me even giving me a very good education.

When his wife tried to maltreat me, he was always there to protect me. He is my dad and I can't wait to be done with school and start repaying him for all he has done for me. "

ANASTESIA

"My neighbor used to be very vibrant and hardworking. After her husband died, the children from his previous marriage chased her out of the house. She decided to rent an apartment in the neighborhood.

One day, she confided in me concerning her ill health. She had a fibroid and was scheduled for surgery in her hometown. She decided to go to her hometown because she needed to be close to her family.

After the surgery, her mental health deteriorated. Her brother decided to bring her back to the city. When I saw her, she had lost a lot of weight. She could no longer recognize people. Her landlord threatened to send her out of his house. Neighbors had to intervene and they decided to look for someone related to her to take her back to the village.

Now, people are beginning to wag their tongues, insinuating that she was into some kind of evil practice and that's why she became insane. I wish we could be less judgemental and more empathetic. I suspect her husband's death and the way she was treated has a part to play in her ill health. I pray she receives the necessary treatment she needs so she can come back to the vibrant self we used to know. "

KAMSO

I have been married for three years with a son. I own a restaurant business that gives me daily income while my husband repairs generators.

Over the years, I have noticed that his business has not been thriving. I told him to close it down and join me in the restaurant business, but he blatantly refused. I pay all our bills, including his shop rent.

My husband knows that I keep some money at home because of the nature of my business and sometimes, he would go there and take out some without informing me. It annoys me and no matter where I keep it, he'll still find it.

One day, I was with his phone when he received a text message. The first part caught my interest and I had to open it to read the full message. It was from a lady asking him to send her money. I asked him who the lady was, but he refused to tell me. I decided to make my findings and discovered she is my husband's mistress. I was heartbroken.

How can I be here working hard to sustain the family and all he does is squander the money on another woman. We quarreled over it but in the end, I had to let go for my own peace of mind.

Now, he wants me to have another child for him even when he's not able to care for our first child. I have told him that it wouldn't work and if he does not change his attitude, I will leave him."

JENNY

"I'm from Benue State and I'm a 26 year old graduate. I have been dating this guy for 3 and half years and I love him.

The issue he has is that he doesn't last in bed , not even up to a minute, which is why I have had a heart to heart conversation with him.

I told him he needed to seek medical attention or go for herbal drugs, but he insisted that he's okay.

I'm human and I'm not a saint. The truth is I'm scared he is hiding something.

I called him and told him that since he refused to go for treatment, I wouldn't continue with the relationship as it feels like he doesn't care.

He is saying he wants to marry me, yet he doesn't want to seek medical attention.

I am confused."

GRACE

"In August, my colleague at work asked me for help. She said someone used juju on her mom, which damaged her left leg.

I had 90k I saved for my house rent which was going to expire in October. Sincerely, I felt for her. Out of my kind heart, I gave her 90k. I explained to her what the money was for and she promised to pay back. She even swore to return it to me before that October and I believed her.

She took permission from work and left for the village. She is from Nsukka. A week later, I called to check on her and the mum, to know if she's responding to treatment.

After 2 weeks, this girl refused to pick my call again. I have tried different numbers. I sent messages, but she didn't pick up. No response from her even till today.

I went to where she was staying with her boyfriend and I explained everything to the guy. He told me that he didn't have any business again with her.

Please I really need advice. If there's another way I can reach this girl and get my money from her. I don't know where she is from in Nsukka. My landlord is on my neck and I'm now hiding to enter my room.

The other day he locked my room. I begged him to allow me. That before ending, I'd pay him. I don't know how to get this girl. I never knew she would be this heartless towards me. "

AYO

"When we were dating, my mother never liked her and she made it very clear to me. I took it as just a woman to woman dislike and continued with her to the point of marriage.

My mother was unhappy with my decision but in the end, there was nothing she could do. I didn't have a good job then so after marriage, we continued to stay in my family house. My wife knew this was going to happen because we talked about it. The plan was to start off there while I got myself together to rent a place of our own.

It wasn't long after the marriage that she started bickering over our moving out. Surprisingly, my mother didn't have any issues with her. They may not like each other, but they were not quarreling or fighting over anything.

We were still there when we had our first child. All through our stay, my mother was very supportive both financially and in taking care of our child.

Eventually, we moved out. Even then, my mother was still very supportive and practically took care of the bills for our children. Things went well for a while, then a couple of years later, she started complaining again that we should move out of that house to another.

When I ignored her, she started misbehaving. She would go and return when she liked. We were lucky my mother was not so far from us, so I could always take the children to her.

I complained to her family but nothing good came out of it. Even my mother tried to talk to her but that was like putting fuel to the fire.

I came back from work one day to find out she had moved out. The kids were with my mother then. After several family meetings, she returned.

Not long after, she moved out again. I would have ignored her if not for the fact that she went with the children. After they returned, I decided to give in to her request and rented a new and bigger place. I thought this would settle our quarrels, but her attitude didn't change.

Since she had her own room in the house, it meant we didn't get to spend time as husband and wife. She would go out and leave the children to themselves. She got a job and I only got to find out from my children.

Recently, I came back from work to find my house deserted. She had moved out again with the children. I am so angry I don't even know what to do. One thing I'm sure of is that I won't be making any attempt at bringing her back.

It is obvious she is tired of the marriage and I am also tired of the drama. I only feel bad for my children who are caught in all these. It's hard sometimes to look my mother in the face, while I tell her what's happening because she warned me and I went my own way. "

MARK

"I had been working in the company for 4 years before they employed some people through their Graduate Trainee programme.

She was one of the new employees and we quickly became friends. Sometimes, she would come to my house to spend the weekend. Other times, we would go to clubs to unwind.

On that fateful day, we went to the club. We drank and I was a bit tipsy, but we got home safely. While I was in my room, she walked in and undressed before me. I was aroused and attempted to kiss her, but she resisted the first attempt. However, she yielded when I tried again and that led to intercourse.

The next day, she called to say I raped her and that if I denied it, she'd produce evidence to prove it. I didn't know she had made a video of us making out.

She reported me to her brother who demanded that I should pay some money otherwise they'd get me arrested. I tried explaining to him that it was consensual, but he refused to believe me. I was still taking it as a minor issue that we'd resolve when the next day, she brought her brother and some policemen to the office to arrest me.

The case escalated to us getting lawyers involved. Eventually, we all agreed to settle out of court. I was already distraught with people's perception of me and the fact that my job was at stake. I thought paying them would solve the problem, so we agreed on a lesser amount which I paid.

Unfortunately, the company already made their decision and my employment was terminated. While I lost my job, she's still working there acting the hero. I feel terrible for falling into her trap and I know one day, I will be vindicated."

EFOSA

"My mom left me when I was just two weeks old.
She is over 50 now and I'm 31, yet she hasn't asked about me or my whereabouts.

I'm an only child. I graduated with a B.sc in mass communication in 2015. I have tried so many times to get a job but all proves futile.

Currently, I have a teaching job which pays me 18, 000 naira monthly. I have been managing it.

Sometimes I get 1000 naira electrical jobs. I have no choice but to do it to survive .

I pray to God to give me a good job so I can eat a decent meal for once ."

BLESSING

"My heart is heavy and I just feel like letting it all out here. My husband and I got married 2 years ago. He had a little job he was managing then and I was also into content writing.

His boss suddenly started owing him for months. We had to rely on the less than 50k monthly I was making from ghostwriting.

He confided in a distant cousin who advised him to relocate to PH. He promised to help him secure a good job as soon as possible because according to him, there were lots of job opportunities in Port Harcourt.

My husband got excited and we started making plans to relocate to PH. We engaged the services of an agent and in no time, our apartment was ready.We moved to PH exactly 2 months ago.

When we got here, my husband contacted his cousin. He seemed happy that we finally came. He promised to send his address or come over to our place. That was the last we heard from him. He stopped picking our calls and stopped responding to our messages.

This was someone my husband housed and fed his sister when she was in the higher institution because my husband was living around the school.

When her brother offered to help my husband get a good job, we thought he was about to return the favor. My husband felt betrayed, but I encouraged him to look up to God.

Within these two months, my husband has been seriously job hunting without success. He finally settled for a teaching job of 20k (an Accountant).

Sometimes, I hear him cry to God in the middle of the night. The other night I heard him telling God that he felt less of a man watching me feed our baby pap without milk when he's still alive. It brought tears to my eyes, but I have to be strong for the 3 of us because I observed that he's not all that emotionally strong.

I've been trying my best to encourage and pray for him because I'm very sure that God must surely come through for us. I need all the encouraging words I can get here please.

I don't want to talk to my family or friends about this because I don't want to give anybody the room to look down on my King.

By the grace of God, I'm grateful that we have a roof over our heads and we've never gone to bed on an empty stomach. I feel better now that I've poured out my heart here. "

AMARA

"I'm 20 years old. On 22 of October 2022, I entered a keke. We were actually 4 in the keke— two boys, one girl and myself.

Before I knew what was happening, the keke man followed another route and I was scared. I tried to scream, but I felt this numbness.

When I woke up, I was in a particular place with my clothes tattered. I couldn't process what happened. I had to beg for transport for me to get back home. I didn't say a word to anyone because I grew up in a type of home where communication with your family seems hard, especially my mum,but no one was around.

I'm staying with my brother. I noticed some severe pains in my vagina for almost three days. I didn't really know what to do because I'm learning a trade. I don't have money to check in the hospital. I browsed about it online and saw that what could cause such pain was rape,infections and so on.

On discovering that, I was scared. I almost ran mad, because I don't know how to explain anything to my brother. I tried committing suicide ,that was the only option I had then,but I couldn't be cruel to myself.

I drew closer to God ,I questioned him even though I knew it's foolish. I didn't get myself for up to one week. I spoke to a gynecologist online and he asked for a consultation fee, but I didn't have any. I begged him to just listen to me and advise me on what to do.

After so much pleading, he agreed. I explained everything to him and he suggested I tell my mum and go for an HIV test. I told him I wasn't going to tell my mum because she was in the hospital. Then he said I should go to the hospital first and report the case to the police.

I can't report to the police, because there are no more police in my area. Secondly, I don't have any solid evidence with me, so I just forgot about reporting the case thinking I can overcome it.

Suddenly, I started feeling changes in my body, starting from my breast,I was worried. I had to google it and the result was showing it's a pregnancy symptom or cancer. Just to be sure I bought a pregnancy test kit and it was positive. I couldn't believe it because the other line was not showing clearly.

5 days later, I bought another one and it was confirmed I was pregnant. I don't know what to do. My mum is in the hospital, and my brother is struggling. He won't even believe me if I told him.

I thought of abortion, because if I told my brother he would send me out of the house. But before I thought about the abortion, I looked for a different job I could do to get an apartment to stay and take care of the pregnancy, but I couldn't find one. So I had to google about pills I could take, and was shown two medications called mifepristone and misoprostol.

I decided to go for it even though I didn't want to. I couldn't buy it in the street where we live,so I went to a different pharmacy, but they didn't want to sell it to me. Instead they were asking questions and asking for doctor prescriptions because I was told one of the drugs was for an ulcer patient.

I pleaded, they agreed, but the amount for the drugs was much. I had to borrow money and buy only misoprostol from another place. I used the pillswith prayers,yeah I could be stupid for that,but God knows my heart,I took the pill on a Monday morning. I bled on that day, but for the rest of the week, I had zero to no bleeding.

Suddenly the bleeding started again and up till now I am still bleeding. I googled it and it showed it's normal to bleed for a week or two but deep down inside I had a feeling the pills did not work.

I wanted to go for an ultrasound, but I dont have money. I don't have friends due to what I passed through as a child. And the person I borrowed from, I'm not sure she would give me again since I'm still owing her.

Please, I dont know what else to do. I have asked God for signs but nothing. The only thing on my mind is suicide. I don't know what to do again and time is really going. "

AMINA

"Sometimes I ask myself why good things do not come to the righteous ones. I am living a decent life yet I am suffering.

At my age I'm still struggling financially even though I am decent. I have no good job. I applied for a job, but the person in charge wanted to sleep with me. I refused and that was how I lost the job—a job with a salary of 90k.

Now I'm back to working for a meager salary. Another lady got the job. When I saw the person hiring for the job, I asked him why he refused to give me knowing that I qualified for it. He said "but you refused to do what your mates are doing," I felt so bad and cried my eyes out.

I learnt content writing, managing social media accounts but jobs haven't been forthcoming. I decided to use a little of my savings to start an online business, yet men will come to my inbox asking me to deliver the goods to them in their homes. If I refuse, they won't buy.

I showed my goods to one guy, he underpriced it to the extent I was forced to sell it for a little gain. The same person that was offering me money to sleep with him and I refused, why can't he use the money and buy goods from me?

The one I asked to give me money to add to my business, said he doesn't have it. Yet every Sunday, he'd post on his status videos of girls dancing on his laps in clubs and he'd be spraying money on them.

Honestly I'm really tired. Does it mean that decency no longer thrives in this society? No one wants a responsible girl anymore. They'd rather splash money on girls in a club than support a hustling girl. "

EVELYN

"Some months back, I shared a story about my boyfriend of 5yrs and a new suitor recommended by pastors. I confirmed from God, but my parents refused to allow me marry the one I chose.

It hasn't been an easy battle since April, but finally God made a name for himself.

I'm getting married to my boyfriend and I am so happy. My family said he'd need to re-do the introduction as they didn't accept the first one he did.

He accepted and did the introduction again and he also collected the list. We are planning towards a fixed date for the fulfillment of all marital rites and then a ceremony , possibly Easter.

I'm happy and I really appreciate everyone's advice.God did it for me after so many battles. "

CHINELO

"My mother-in-law was an agile woman before she went down with a stroke which has left her incapacitated.She has five children—three boys and two girls. My husband is the second son.

Before she became sick, she had already handed over all her property documents to her last son, the favorite. She has two houses. We all live in one, while the other one is rented out.

Two weeks ago, I was in my room when I heard one of my sisters-in-law screaming . I ran out to inquire what the problem was and I discovered that my mother -in law had messed up herself. I told her to clean her up and stop shouting so as not to attract the attention of the neighbors. She told me she was fed up. Apparently, mama messes up herself on a daily basis, so she was tired because her brother who is in charge of the rent has refused to assist.

My husband, on the other hand, is angry with his mum for giving everything to her last son. I have told my husband not to neglect his mum even though I know he is struggling. Besides, we are living in her house without paying rent. That's something to be grateful for. I wish my brother-in-law would care for his mum from the proceeds he gets from the rent. It's really heartbreaking seeing her suffering when she has children. "

AHMED

"I was just a baby when my mum abandoned me with my blind father. Since my dad could not take care of me because of his predicament, my uncle took me to his house.

My dad died when I was eight years old. Since then, things have not been the same. My uncle's wife treats me like an outcast. Though they have kids older than me, I do all the domestic chores at home, including going to the market. Despite all these, my uncle never cautions her.

After I graduated from secondary school, I decided to write JAMB exams even when it was not clear my uncle would sponsor my tertiary education.

While waiting for the result, I decided to get a job. My plan was to save some money that might come in handy when I get admission. My uncle's wife was not happy because I was no longer at home running errands for her.

Two weeks ago, I received an email that I've been offered admission to study law. I was elated. When I got home I told my uncle and his wife, but I could read from their body language that they were not happy.

Two days ago, I overheard my uncle's wife telling him that she was not happy that I was doing better than their son. That statement broke my heart, but I've decided not to dwell on it.

I have told my aunty about my admission and she has promised to support me with the little she can. She too is struggling.

Right now, I am not letting any negative thoughts in my head, I am just happy to be leaving home soon and believe that everything will work out in the end."

VICTORY

"I am a single mom of a 3 year old son.

I got pregnant at age 18. I met my son's father on 3rd January, 2018. He was a NEPA staff member, while I was learning a skill. We started dating.

Later on, he started requesting for sex. When I refused, he asked for a breakup.

I started begging because he was my first love.

Then in the month of April, I told him that if having sex with him would keep the relationship, then I was going to do it.

He took my virginity in April with the promise of never leaving me. Being a kid then, I believed every one of his words.

Even made me to always have sex with him every Sunday night except the time I was menstruating.

Each time I said no, he would get angry with me till I agreed to have sex with him.

In the month of September, he started behaving strangely towards me. I caught him in bed with a lady he claimed to be his friend. He apologized that day and we ended up having sex again. How foolish I was.

In October, he called me and said he wanted us to break up and stop having sex because he was no longer interested . I begged, he refused and I moved on.

I never knew I was even more than 5 months pregnant because my stomach was very flat, till I went to the hospital.

My mom summoned him. At first he denied ,the next day he apologized and accepted with the agreement that he would be taking responsibility.

He took responsibility from when he knew I was pregnant till my son was 7 months old because he said he wanted to go to school.

With the help of my mom, I took care of my son because I left him at 2 months with my mom, while I was going to work.

When my son's father told me he'd be going back to school, I was happy for him. Only for him to say I should take my 10 months old child to his family house which I refused.

Then his mom started having issues with me because I refused to allow my son to stay with them. I took care of my son's bill for 2yrs plus without his support.

Fast forward to last year, I got admission. But when it was time to collect my money from the woman I was doing esusu(daily contributions) with, I found out she had run. This drove me into depression.

I had to take my son to his father's family with the agreement that he'd be coming down to Abuja every holiday.I took him there last December. He was 2 yrs, 10 months then.

In March, he was supposed to visit but because the holiday was too short, I decided to leave for the long holiday in July .

Around April this year, I told his dad that I would like my son to come visit for a long holiday. His reply was that my son can't come to Abuja for the next 7 years. I told him that was not our agreement and asked why the change of plans. He said he had spoken already. That if I'd like to see him, I should be traveling down to Kaduna.

In may/June, I kept begging him to allow my son to come visit, but he refused. I called his mom and she said she had nothing to say, that I should talk to my son's father.

Since he refused to allow my son to visit, I came up with a plan. They never knew my intention was to come and pick my son and run away. I told them I had a program in Kaduna. When I got there, I took my son because he was too tender and he was not experiencing any love there.

My son was calling me aunty and calling his father's sister mummy. He looked so lean.

In August, I told his father about his school fees and he said I should never call him for anything again.

After 1 month, he called and said he wanted to talk to his son. I agreed because I felt he had come back to his senses. I started allowing him to talk to him on the phone.

My son became very sick in October 2022, and I was yet to receive my salary. I called him to send some money to take him to the hospital or buy drugs for him. But he said I should handle it on my own, since I ran away with him and hung up the phone.

After three days, he called and asked to speak with him. But I refused since he didn't help out when he was sick. I have asked him to stop calling me till he's ready to take responsibility.

I need the help of a welfare officer or any concerned organization so he can choose between taking care of his responsibilities or never to bother me again. "

STANLEY

"I met a beautiful lady I wanted to marry. We both worshiped in the same church, so the counseling process was not as tedious as it would have been for non-members.

During one of the meetings, the main pastor who was a white man said he would assign the assistant pastor, a Nigerian, to us since he knew our culture and traditions better than him.

I was not comfortable with the arrangement since the assistant pastor was single, but I continued with it.

One day, I was in the church when the pastor announced the marriage between my fiancee and the assistant pastor. I was shocked. Everybody knew we were getting married. I was heartbroken and depressed.

It's been a long time, but I've not been able to get over that ugly incident. Getting a wife now has become an uphill task for me. I have engaged 3 different women at different times but even after meeting their families, I end up breaking off the relationship."

TITI

"I was told his wife had died four years earlier and he was now ready to marry another.

As a pastor, it wasn't proper for him to stay single. It was my own pastor that introduced us. When we met, he hardly spoke and I just took it that he was the quiet type.

After that first meeting, he hardly called and since we were in different states, visiting was difficult too.

We went ahead to start marriage plans. I had my doubts, but my pastor told me he was a good man and I should be patient with him.

We met a few more times before the marriage. I never visited him all through the period.

The wedding was in my state and I had naturally assumed I'd move in with him and prepared my things. He never said anything about it and I didn't see it as a problem.

I was surprised when on our wedding night, he told me he'd go back alone and come and take me later. I was angry, but I didn't want us to quarrel, so I let it be.

When I eventually joined him, it was in a new apartment. I knew he lives in the church premises but rather than take me there, he rented a new place.

Some days he'd stay in the church house, while on other days, he'd come home.

I have never entered the house but those who frequent it tell me he still has his late wife's picture and other things the way they were before she died.

I had tried to ignore all these, but I do not find it funny anymore. The one that annoyed me the most happened recently. It was the anniversary of his wife's death and he put up her picture on his WhatsApp status.

If it was just one day, I wouldn't have minded so much. But he kept it on for over a week, uploading different pictures without a care for how I feel.

At this point, I'm not sure he has gotten over her or if he ever will and I cannot continue like this."

BUNMI"

"I'm a single mum. My son is 5 years old. I got pregnant when I was 18,that was when I lost my virginity to Dad. He wasn't in Nigeria then, so I was with my mum suffering with the pregnancy.

We barely had food to eat. I struggled with my mum till my elder sister took my mum and I to Aba where she's staying. She took care of me and registered me at the hospital.

He wasn't calling me till my 8th month. He said that he had issues where he was, but he's back. I directed him to my sister's place in Aba. He came with the sister and said he wanted me to come to his place and stay. My sister told him that it wasn't the right way to do things. She asked them to go, that I'd come see him later.

He left with the sister without even asking me how I was doing. After some weeks, we went to my mum's place because it's close to his place. My uncles invited him and his people. They came and he agreed he's the father of the baby.

After a long discussion, we agreed that I'd stay at my mum's place till I put to bed.

Because of that, he wasn't giving me money for upkeep. I chatted him up and ask him how we were going to buy things for the baby. He said he'd give the sister money to go buy them. I asked him why he'd give the sister some money instead of me, but he ended the call.

Before then, my sister had gotten everything I needed for delivery and for the baby too. He wasn't even coming to see me till the day of my delivery. He took me to the hospital and I delivered successfully.

I stayed at his place with his mum and my mum too. He wasn't greeting my mum. He would hit his mum whenever she asked him why he went out and didn't come back. He was always going out without coming back.

His mum was the one taking care of our feeding and everything. I told the mum that I would like to go, that I couldn't deal with his behavior. The mum told his Dad and they agreed. My uncle came to pick us up and his mum told me that she'd be coming to see us.

The day this thing was happening, he wasn't around. The father called him on the phone to come. He said he was coming. We waited for him for an hour, but he didn't come. He said I should leave his son for him, since I was going.

We left his place at my dad's place in Umuahia. My sister rented an apartment for me and my baby. He was 3 months old then. He started calling me on the phone threatening me to bring back his son. I told him we were at my dad's place. I asked him to come see his baby anytime he wanted.

The day he came to my dad's place with his friends, we were not there. He saw only my Dad and told him he was there to pick his son. My dad told him that we were not around. He requested for them to have a conversation. He started insulting my dad and was shouting at his place before leaving with his friends.

Later, he called me on the phone and insulted my family and I. He said I should keep the boy, that he won't take care of him till I bring him back to him. I told him I wasn't keeping his son away from you, he could see him anytime he wanted, but I can't give my baby to him because he's still small.

He stopped calling both his people and I. I later took him to welfare. They invited him and asked what I did to him. He said I did nothing to him, that he's behaving that way because I didn't want to marry him. I told them I wouldn't marry him because of his behavior and that I was not yet ready for marriage.

Secondly he's toxic, so he should be taking care of his son and forget about me. I planned to stay with my son till he's old enough to speak for himself. He said he'd put him in school and send 15, 000 naira every month for his upkeep. We accepted.

From then till now we haven't heard from him. He didn't put him in school and he didn't send money for upkeep. I have been taking care of my son alone with my sister. Now he is no longer going to school because there's no money for his school fees.

My mum is sick and I'm the one taking care of her. Since I lost my job, things have been very difficult for us. We barely feed. I don't know what to do now. I'm confused. I don't want to ruin his future. Should I take him back to his father?

He is no longer going to school. I'm doing an online business that's where we're feeding from. I acquired a baking skill but I don't have anything to start working with.

I'm losing it, I don't know what to do again. Since I lost my dad, no one is helping me out. My sister is in her finals in school and now things are difficult for her too. She can't see herself through school and be taking care of my son and I. I am 23 years old now, but I have not gone to the university."

BELLO

"I was born in a small village in Kogi State. Having completed my education, I moved to Abuja in 2009 and ever since then, it has been from one job to the other.

The only time I ever had a sigh of relief was when I got married in 2014. Thereafter, it has been a serious battle for survival for life. Though, I was blessed with two kids but then we lived in agony.

All my efforts to make life meaningful has yielded no result. Even when I am on my best behavior, I still get battered. People disrespect me just because I want to see everyone as my friend or brother.

Now the last one came from a friend I'm currently supporting for House of Reps. This call came because I have a gift of dreams.

When I dreamt about him vying for the position, I told him that I saw him in the national assembly as a rep member, and that he should consider running for the position.He looked at me, shook his head and said he didn't have the finances. I told him that was what I saw and as the days passed, I visited to remind him to take my dream seriously.

In 2020, I told him I had already created a platform on social media to galvanize for him. He frowned at it and said it was too early even if he were to be interested. I replied and said a journey of a thousand miles begins with a single step.

Day after day, I continued to do my awareness. Three months into my activities, he called to inform me he had also prayed and he was told to run. So, we started the movement.

We talked about the party because where we come from is predominantly PDP and APC is the party at the helm of affairs. After much deliberation, I suggested for him to go for PDP even though it is an opposition party in the state.

My faith was renewed as we started planning on how to raise funds. Though he's into real estate, he was not really well known. And that's all he had at the time.

Today, we had already won party primaries despite having to contend with party structure and big men who are not just rich in pocket but also in experience.

But having won the primaries, the war between us started. It became apparent that his people felt since I am not from the same community, they needed to drag me far away because to them, I'm beginning to become too close to the decision making process.

Even on his part, he doesn't see me as a friend anymore. All my effort to see he emerged is being submerged by other close friends and family. His wife throws jabs at me whenever she pleases and he'd justify her actions.

One day, I called him to talk and ask what have I done to deserve those harsh treatment from him, his wife, and his other friends. He apologized and said he noticed some of the treatment but never knew it was that bad. Hence, promised to address the situation.

Days after, I noticed some little changes and I was happy. Little did know that it won't last.

After a while, everything becomes a charade. I'm no longer put in the know about major things.

While we were still working on the campaign, I successfully introduced my people in our two wards. Their support would have amounted to about 29, 000 votes should they decide to vote for him in the forthcoming elections.

However, I no longer enjoy any close relationship with him. Anytime I try to introduce a subject like that, he would diplomatically ignore it and say we should talk about this later.

At this point, I'm confused, I feel dejected and used but going back to my people to say they can't work for him will cost so much having committed financially, morally and even spiritually. Not forgetting the sacrifices we have made for the movement in the constituency.

At this point , I have committed everything I have to the cause. I have nothing now. My hope had always been that if this scales through, I would end up with a better life. But now it seems the hope has been dashed. I have a family to feed and fees to pay. I don't know where to go from here. It seems I'm back to square one after all my sacrifices. I feel pained and disappointed."

MIRIAM

"I was in secondary school when I met my husband. My elder brother brought me to the city, so I could attend a better school.

I had lived in the village most of my life and wasn't very comfortable with the city life. What made it worse was that my brother was unmarried then and wasn't the outgoing type. He also lived in a secluded neighborhood so there was usually no one to talk to.

At the new school which was the one of the best in the area, I didn't fit in and was uncomfortable. Soon, I started skipping school. My brother usually left for work very early and returned late at night.

Instead of going to school, I'd take a stroll around the neighborhood. I made friends in different places I could visit whenever I wanted. That was how I met my husband and we started dating.

When my brother found out I was skipping school, he tried advising me to change. When that didn't work he resorted to threats, but I wasn't moved. There was nothing much he could do as he still had to leave for work everyday and left me at home alone.

When it was obvious I wouldn't change, he sent me back to the village. By then, I felt I was old enough to fend for myself. I would leave the village to the city to visit my boyfriend.

Then I got pregnant. When my brother heard, he was very angry and refused to have anything to do with me. I eventually moved in with my boyfriend and fortunately for me, he and his family decided to come pay my bride price.

When I gave birth, my brother still refused to come see me. It took years before we reconciled. I have four children now and he's the one taking full responsibility for their schooling. He has also promised to put them through the university so long as they're willing.

My problem now is my husband. He has refused to do any work. I have complained and gotten different people to talk to him. Even my brother has suggested businesses for him to do, but he doesn't want to lift a finger.

If not for the fact that we live in his family house and do not pay rent, I don't know how we would have coped. I am the one fending for the family. Our feeding, clothing, everything is on me.

To meet up, I do my business everyday, come rain come shine. Even on this one, he doesn't help. I struggle with my older children just to make sure the business keeps moving.

What keeps me is the fact that he's not violent. If he had as much as raised his hands on me any day, I would have left. Since we can still live in peace, I focus on my children and my business and take my life as punishment for being foolish when I was younger."

JOSHUA

"When I started worshiping in the church in my area, I became committed to being a worker. It's been 3 years since I started going to this Church.

6 months ago, a sister in the Lord and her husband approached me to join the contribution they were doing. 50,000 naira every month. I asked around and about 5 members were also doing it, so I joined.

I never failed to remit my money every month. I thought I was dealing with someone in the church seeing how this sister and her husband were very committed in church.

It's my turn to receive this October and I sent my account details. Little did I know that this woman had run away with my money. My hard earned 300,000 naira.

First they packed out from where they used to live. I was able to locate their new apartment, but they were nowhere to be found. Their phones are switched off. Worst is that other people are also looking for them for the same reason. I heard that someone even broke the husband's head.

I trusted these people because I met them in church. Honestly I don't feel like attending church anymore. I labored to save this money, deprived myself of so many things just to save. I don't even know how to locate them."

SOLA

"I was born normal. I walked like other children. Then, as an adolescent, they said, I fell. They didn't think it was serious, so, no medical care was given.

That was how I became disabled. A disability that has left me with constant back pain.

After secondary school, I found a job selling products for a company. It was hell. My wheelchair was always faulty. My mom was alone with 8 children while my dad had passed on. I managed to save, took JAMB and got admission.

My woes began, I'd go to people, plate in hand, begging for fees from anywhere possible.

Now I'm about to graduate, the project is still hanging and this session fees are hanging.

To add to my woes, the rainy season destroyed my wheelchair because of getting stuck in the mud.

Coming to a relationship? Hmm, who wants a liability? So, I've just zeroed my mind on a life, alone."

ADEKUNLE

"I am currently a final year student in the university. I really struggled to see myself through secondary school, since I came from an average background. It wasn't easy for me then. But by God's grace I later made it out of there by doing some menial Jobs and cultivating for people.

After I graduated from secondary school, I started moving from city to city—struggling and trying my best.

In 2017 one of my uncles told me to forget about traveling and instead, get a Jamb form that he would sponsor me in the university. I invested the little money I had then towards this plan.

Later,I got the admission. Unfortunately, he abandoned me after my 100 level. I had to take up the responsibility of training myself by doing some jobs.

However, in my final year things became extremely worse and I have not been able to raise my school fee as I used to do before.

As it stands now, I have been frústrated and depressed as I watch others go through their final year process, while I mourn privately. I have been able to raise some part of it. I don't want to drop out now."

OGHOSA

"I was in my apartment when my friend called me to follow her to go see someone. I readily accepted, since I wasn't doing anything. The guy came to pick us and we went out to chill. On our way, I noticed that he was driving towards the outskirts of the city and I wondered why.

As if he read my mind, he told us he wanted to go to a bush bar, because he wanted something very local for the evening. My friend and I said okay. He kept driving far away from the main town.

We finally got to the place and it was truly a local bar with local delicacies. We made our order and ate.

After eating and it was time to go home, the guy insisted that we must follow him to his house, but I refused. I told them that I'd be going to work the next day as I was on morning duty. I said I was going home, while my friend should go with her guy.

But my friend insisted she won't follow him. I told her to follow him. Only then did she tell me that she hadn't met him before, that that was their first meeting. They had been chatting on the phone. I told her to sort herself out and that I must go back home.

The man kept insisting we must follow him. After a series of back and forth, he agreed to drop us. We went back into his car and he started driving into the bush. We became alarmed. Worst still, he started making strange calls.

My friend and I jumped out of the moving vehicle. It was in the bush as the car wasn't moving fast and it was dark too.We ran and hid while he tried to find us, but he didn't. He started driving out of the bush.We went home after he left. I don't know what could have happened to us that night."

JOHNSON

"My younger sister was sent on an errand by our mom to buy something in the neighborhood. After hours of waiting without seeing her, we became worried.

My mom decided to go to the shop she had sent her to. The shop owner said my sister left immediately.

We searched for her for days, but she was nowhere to be found.

My mother was against reporting the matter to the Police. She didn't trust them to do anything. She rather decided to visit a prophet who had just moved into the neighborhood. The prophet told my mum to pray and fast for three days, and at the end of the fast, my sister would be found. This was in addition to money and other things we were required to provide.

At the end of the fast, the prophet sent for my mum. When she got to his house, he told her that God had revealed to him exactly where my sister was. My mum sent for my siblings and other members of the family. When we got to the place we were directed to by the prophet, my sister was right there, in a bush in the neighborhood. Just sitting all by herself.

We have since been trying to get her to tell us what happened, but she doesn't seem to remember. She didn't even act like she had been missing for days or she had been in the bush all the while. Though we suspect that the prophet had a hand in her disappearance, we have decided to let her be and hope that one day we will get the truth of what happened. We are just happy that she is back to us. "

CHIZITERE

"I once shared a story here about my polygamous family earlier this year and how I was homeless in Lagos between 2005, 2006, 2007, 2008 till late 2009.

I later rented a one room apartment in a face-me-I-face-you compound in Lagos.

I was not given any room in the six rooms bungalow that my father built in the village. My late mother was the second wife. And out of the six rooms in the bungalow, only two rooms were given to my mom. When she died, the rooms were given to my two oldest brothers.

I tried protesting about it. I talked to my oldest brother and he told me to calm down and instead take his own room. He said I didn't know what the future would hold—I might end up building my own house.

I took his advice, cried to God about it and God Almighty heard my cry. This coming December, by the special grace of God Almighty, I will be opening my house in the village. A very beautiful house that no one in my family has built.

I have called my oldest brother to inform him that officially that we would be moving into our own house built by me this December.

I didn't even build the house on our own land, I bought the land. In addition, I will also be buying a house in Lagos by the grace of God this December.

I'm sharing this to encourage, motivate and also to tell someone who will read this post to be patient with God. There's God and he sees everything."

DIMEJI

"Anytime I see the police searching a young man, I always feel sorry and worried for him. This is because that young man might end up being accused for what he knows nothing about.

Though I have been lucky, I know people who haven't been so lucky. I learn from their experiences to avoid trouble.

My closest shave happened one day. I was just returning from visiting a relative with two other relatives in the car with me. I was stopped at a checkpoint and asked for the usual particulars, which I provided.

The policeman then went further to ask for a Road Worthiness Certificate. I told him my car was for private use and I thought the certificate was required for only commercial vehicles. He said since I didn't have it, I'd have to follow him to the station.

Before we could even argue, he had ordered the person seated in front to get down and he got in the front seat. I wasn't willing to part with any money as a bribe so at his command, I drove to the station which wasn't very far from the checkpoint.

Fortunately for me, I knew a high ranking officer so I called him. He asked to speak with the officer and in no time, I was asked to leave. The same policeman pleaded that I let him join me back to the checkpoint. I refused because I didn't trust him. The people with me felt sorry for him and asked that I let him join us. Again, he insisted on sitting in front. I was watching him all the way because I suspected he was up to something.

Just as we approached the checkpoint, I saw him lift his shirt, brought out bullets and was about to put them in my pigeonhole when I immediately held his hands. Those behind only realized what was happening when they noticed our struggle and the vehicle swerving and almost ran into a ditch.

As the vehicle came to a halt right in front of the checkpoint, I still held him because I knew once I let him go, he might drop the bullets in the car. I even had to follow him through the passenger door so as not to let go of him.

There was another officer there of higher rank and we immediately raised the alarm. Whether they were working together or not, I cannot tell but that one quickly apologized for his colleague's behavior and told us to go.

My brothers with me were sorry they made me carry him. Imagine if I had not caught him, he would have dropped those bullets and then at the checkpoint, he'd insist on searching me again and I'd be branded a criminal.

Since then, I am extra careful and watchful when a policeman is searching my car or in the vehicle with me. I also tell anyone who cares to listen to do the same."

BUKOLA

"I once had a chemist shop that was thriving very well. Almost everyone in my vicinity patronized me because I was the only one selling medication then.

One day, a lady who was very close to me came seeking financial assistance for her friend. At first, I didn't want to give her the money since I was not familiar with the third party, but she assured me that she would pay if her friend defaulted. I gave her the amount she asked for which I had kept for my shop rent.

When it was time to return my money as agreed, it became a problem. I would call, send texts all to no avail. Meanwhile, my rent was due for renewal. I had to use the money I kept for restocking to renew the rent.

Things became rough for me. My shop was almost empty. I became sick and had a stroke. That was how I lost my business.

Now, I'm struggling to raise money to start up again. I have also learnt my lesson."

JENNIFER

"When I started my online business last year, my hubby tried to talk me out of it. He said I was stressing myself out. He took care of the kids and I very well and provided for everything. He told me not to bother myself and just relax. But I continued doing the business in my own little way not wanting to back down.

Few months back, armed robbers started attacking the place we used to live and we needed to pack out as soon as possible. My hubby paid for rent, including agent fees. Everything amounted to 510, 000, naira. Some of the jobs he did haven't been paid for and we were left with no savings.

Since then, I have been the one catering for the family from the savings from my business. And in this economy, no one is ready to lend anyone any money.

My little baby and I had malaria,so I comfortably brought out money for her treatment.

I have been running the house expenses. My husband is shocked and proud at the same time. He promised to give me money when they pay for the contracts he did. Even if he doesn't pay me back, as a woman, I know how to collect the money back, and save it again.

I'm happy seeing the smiles on his face whenever I tell him not to worry about what we would eat. And he doesn't have to go around borrowing money."

MARY

When I married my husband, it was his idea that I should resign from my job so I could take care of the children. I tried to talk him out of it but to no avail.

Six years later, after we've had two children, he started misbehaving. He would complain about everything. He became irritated with my presence.

Sometimes when he's talking and I would try to make an input, he would hush me, telling me to keep quiet because according to him, my accent was terrible. That he didn't want me to influence the children with it. Sometimes he would scold me in their presence.

I had to look for a job. I got a teaching job in my children's school. One day, I overheard my colleagues talking about me.Apparently, my husband was cheating on me with one of the caregivers. I couldn't stand the shame and humiliation. So, I resigned and relocated to my state with my children.

I have gotten a better job and I'm glad I left. It was the best decision I ever made."

MATTHEW

"I am 24 years old. I used to have a girlfriend. We hung out often, had fun and all.

All of a sudden, I started noticing some changes in her attitude towards me. Our relationship was sexual as well. Bottom line, I caught her cheating.

When I asked why she did it, she told me that I was too huge for her and she needed something smaller. We had to break up.

Now, the same thing is about to happen in my present relationship. My girlfriend complains about my manhood being too much for her, that it wasn't what she bargained for. I don't even know what to do again.

I find older ladies extremely attractive—Ladies in their late twenties, thirties and even forties. I've had flings with them and they have all said the same thing. I didn't give it much thought then as I knew it was just a fling.

But now that I'm trying to build something serious with someone, it has become concerning for me because the ladies are complaining about it so much."

HOPE

"My mum died when I was ten years old. I had two siblings who were in their teens, struggling to fend for themselves since my mum was not financially stable.

My dad, on the other hand, was not in the picture. He left when I was still a baby. I cannot tell what he looks like.

Two years after my mum's death, a lady came to see my siblings. She offered to take care of me, but my siblings were reluctant because they felt she would maltreat me since we were not related. I told them I would go with the lady to ease off the burden they carried.

When I got to her house, the lady treated me well. She provided me with everything I needed and even sent me to school.

After I graduated from secondary school, she asked me to choose a skill I would like to learn. I opted for fashion design. She paid the necessary fees and I began my apprenticeship.

Today, I own a shop with people working under me. If it wasn't for her, I don't know what my life would have been like. I'll forever be grateful to her."

UNYIM

"When I was in my 300 level, my dad stopped sponsoring me in school. He practically told me not to mention anything about my welfare to him. I did not do anything wrong to him.

His siblings kept telling him lies about me because their own children have refused to be useful. They even said I was sponsoring a guy in school, which I wasn't.

I was so in pain and depressed. It was only my mom that supported me. She borrowed money to see to it that I finished my studies. My dad even closed her business.

When I was posted for my National Youth service, my dad did not care. It was only God that helped me throughout my 1 year service.

I had to give my mom the money I saved from there to pay back the people she borrowed from.

Now I'm looking for a job. I have a business idea to start but no money. My dad treats me like an outsider,but I'm his only daughter.Before I went for service, I begged him to help me pay for a skill. He refused and said he'd rather pay for my younger brother to learn the skill which he did.

I just pray I get a job fast or start my business because I'm living like a stranger in my father's house. All he talks about is marriage and I am only 24."

MIRACLE
Part 1

" I was born as a second child into the family of five.My parents have this strong hatred for me from birth. I was told that when I was born, things went bad for them. According to them, they moved back to the village, So I was blamed for their predicament.

I wasn't sent to school as a child. At age 6,I was made to look after my younger ones. My younger and elder siblings went to the best nursery and primary schools in Benin.

When I protested, they allowed me to attend an afternoon school.

Before then, I had experienced so many molestations as a result of staying at home.

At age 8, I started wondering why I should stay at home, while my younger and elder siblings were going to school. I started fighting for my right and each time, they'd remind me I was the cause of their problem.

I was always crying. My elder sis was praised, their first son was an angel, and I remained the bad egg.

I became violent as a child because no one wanted to hear me out . They utilized every opportunity to get rid of me. A family member once visited us and said she felt strange things around her at night, that she needed one of their children to be with her for the week. Immediately, my parents offered me to her. I was very happy. At least I would stay away from them. The hate was too much.I was not perfect, but I was a good child. None of my siblings showed me any love.

There was a time my elder sister ran away from home. My parents almost went mad looking for it. When she finally returned, they celebrated and treated her like their gold.

My brother ran away also and the same thing happened.

When I planned my own escape , no member of my family looked for me. They carried on with their normal activity. I was heartbroken. The day I returned, my mum saw me and said her pot of soup would no longer last,that a witch had returned.

I attempted suicide twice. When they found out, my dad and mum said those options of suicide were not effective, that the fastest way was to stand on a major road for a car would crush me.

I started praying to God .I made plans to attend a university. My cut off mark was not good, but I prayed for my name to be among the 3rd badge and God did it. That was how I left that wicked home. My parents were training me in the university before I got married.

Years later, I prayed to God to give me a good husband and he did. He promised to marry me and take me away from them. He came, paid my bride price, and we did our wedding. My husband helped me complete my university education.

I thought my hubby loved me, that luck has finally smiled on me. After one year of my marriage, my hubby started cheating on me with a girl in my street. He married me as a virgin. He knew I was naive. I had never been to Lagos before getting married.

Hubby's girlfriend dealt with me. She'd come with her fellow Edo babes to beat me up. They'd beat and call me ashawo(prostitute).

I lost my self esteem in the process. I knelt down and pleaded with my husband to remember all I have been through. That my family would mock me, but he didn't care.

Eventually,I ran away from them and started staying in our church. My hubby didn't look for me knowing full well I didn't have anybody. Going back home was the last option."

Part 2

"When I couldn't continue staying in the church, I went back home to tell my parents. My mum asked if I preferred her maltreatment of me or my husband's. I was not surprised by the question.

My younger brother came home and started asking that hope I didn't come back home to disturb his parents. Before I could say a word, he started beating and slapping me with the help of my dad. All I saw was my load flying around in the air.

I picked up my stuff and left home to nowhere. Life became worse . I called my hubby and asked him to forgive me. He came, picked me up, and took me back to Lagos.

Life became worse and terrible. Till date, he still cheats on me. Life has never been fair to me. I don't know what to do. I have two kids now. I have a business, but it is not stable. I am just managing myself. I would have moved on, but I don't have the money and I don't have the zeal to continue.

I now believe what my parents said about me. I have prayed, fasted and hoped in God for a miracle, yet. Even my siblings usually remind me that I pray more than everyone but suffers more.

I am on an antidepressant drug because of this. I also have fibromyalgia. I am just struggling to push because of my boys .

Am I truly a witch? Why have I been going through hell from birth? I have lost a son and none of my family visited me."

BOLA

"I was in a relationship with a lady I wanted to marry. We dated for three years. I went to see her family and made my intentions known. Because I wasn't financially stable,I asked them to give me one year to put things in place.

In the course of our dating, I discovered that she was an alcoholic. I would give her money for upkeep and she would spend it on alcohol. Most times when I visited her and vice versa, she would always be at a bar drinking. I told her how uncomfortable I was and she promised to change.

Sometimes, she would exhibit some nasty attitude, but I didn't allow it to affect my love for her.

One fateful day, I was out with my friends, and we got talking. During our conversation, one of them told me that my girlfriend said I was impotent. I was hurt. I decided to confront her, but she denied it. I did not believe her because I knew she was very flippant with words. At that moment, my love for her started to diminish.

Three months later, I met another lady who got pregnant for me and I decided to marry her. Sometimes people make you do things you wouldn't normally do. "

SCHOLASTICA

"I want to share my story concerning premarital sex. I hope people will learn from my mistakes.

It all started in 2009/2010. Immediately after I finished writing my WAEC exams, I met my husband. But before I met him, I had decided on no sex before marriage. My reason being that since I am the first daughter, I wouldn't want to have a child out of wedlock.

I also promised God that if I should get pregnant mistakenly, I wouldn't abort. But if I make an attempt to abort it, he should take my life on the spot.

After meeting my husband, then boyfriend, I told him about the no sex before marriage policy. Initially, he accepted it. But after some time, he started demanding for sex.

By then I had started loving him and I was afraid to lose him. I had to give in to his demands.

Months later, I became pregnant. When I told him about it, he asked me not to tell anyone. Then he took me somewhere to abort it. I begged, cried and even mentioned my promise to God, but he said that nothing will happen if we ask God for forgiveness afterwards. That's how I ended up breaking my promise to God, but his mercy saved and kept me.

I continued dating him and took in again. This time, he came with a drug to terminate it. I ran as fast as my legs could carry me.

We later got married and did both the traditional and white wedding.

Now, the child he wanted us to terminate, he loves her so much. I have given birth to two other boys due to God's mercy. However, since then, there is this strange sickness that has refused to go. I pray that God will heal me too from this sickness. "

JOY

"My father died when I was 10yrs old. From then till today, my mom and I have been suffering.

I am the first child of the family. Everybody is looking up to me. I am 26 yrs old now. The problem is that I've been struggling to meet up in life to help my siblings, but I don't know if I am cursed.

Since I started doing this boyfriend thing, I have never met someone who is willing to help me. The people I have been meeting in life are people that always complain about money. Sometimes I ask myself why I have not met anybody that can help me because I need help.

I cry everyday, asking myself if I am cursed.

I don't have a brother or uncle who can help me.

Sometimes I feel like God doesn't want me to marry. I have never been in a serious relationship. I am not a bad person, but I always meet unserious people who are not ready to settle down. I am so confused.

Since I started working as a sales girl, I have never gotten a job where they pay me more than 15k. I only find jobs. I have been trying my best. I don't know what to do."

AINA

"When my sister started complaining about her husband's infidelity, I told her to confront him. Let him know that she's aware of what he's doing. She confronted him and he apologized.

Few months later, I got a call from her telling me that her husband was still cheating on her. I told her to pray about it and also report him to someone he respects.

Meanwhile, my sister and her husband had a female mutual friend. Sometimes my sister would confide in her. One fateful day, she called to tell me that a mutual friend had arranged for them to meet a prophet who would solve all her problems. I advised her against it, but she was adamant. I didn't know what happened at the prophet's place because my sister refused to tell me.

After the encounter with the prophet, I never heard from her again. I called many times to check up on her, but she wouldn't take my calls. I just felt that whatever she did had worked for her though I never stopped praying for her.

One Sunday morning, while I was preparing to go to church, my brother-in-law called and said that I should come to his house. I thought something bad had happened to my sister.

When I arrived there, I saw my sister crying with the mutual friend beside her, trying to console her. That was when her husband went into the house and came back with a small black bottle wrapped with a piece of red cloth. He told me he found it in my sister's box. Apparently, that was what the prophet had given her to solve her marital problem. That was how my sister lost her home.

One year later, the mutual friend became the new wife. It was a plan all along by the mutual friend to oust my sister so she could marry her husband. Each time I think about it, I get scared of what women do to themselves these days. "

FESTUS

"During the lockdown, the company I was working for sent us on leave without pay. I just just got married and my wife was not doing anything at the time because she just finished her National Youth service.

It was a very difficult time for us. I didn't know what to do. I reached out to so many people but got no help.

One faithful day, I reached out to a senior colleague. He sent me 5k and asked me to see him the next day, that there's an important issue to discuss.

The following day, I went straight to see him. During our conversation, he asked me to steal some items from the company, that he'd sell them for us to make money to solve our problems.I told him it'd be difficult but because of the situation I was in, I said I was going to think about it.

Not long after that, I went to the office to ask when they'd call us back. They told me that they'd get back to us. I walked around and saw something similar to what this man asked me to steal and I called to inform him. He asked me to snap and send, so I did. He said he'd send someone to collect it from me.

Later, someone called me and said that the man sent him to collect something from me, which I gave to him. Before you know it, security arrested the guy and he told them I was the one that gave him the item. The company sacked 3 of us. I went from the frying pan to the fire.

Life has been so hard for me since then. I can't pay house rent and I can't feed my family anymore. Things are really hard. My career is being threatened. I'm depressed and I am thinking of doing something bad because I have failed myself, my wife and children. I really don't know what to do. "

NKI OSOWO

"I come from a broken home. My mother single-handedly raised my sister and I.

I was made to work in my mother's shop, while my sister was doted on. She attended the best private school up to the university level. I went to a public school.

I used to wonder if she was my biological mother.Sometimes, I would lock myself up in the room and cry my eyes out.

One day, I asked my mum why she treated me differently. She said she was preparing me for a better future. I practically worked to please my mum just like an employee would work to please their boss.

After graduation, I was fully involved in my mum's business, while my sister was gallivanting and squandering every penny she received.

Today, I'm happily married to a man who showers me with the love I never experienced. My mother calls me her backbone because I do almost everything for her. Though I turned out better, I do not like what my mother did and will never treat my children unfairly. "

ELIJAH

"I was scammed of 2.3 million naira last year by my supposed best friend.

He once lived in Angola and he assured me that he's going to help me secure a visa to India. Out of trust, I obliged and he scammed me.

I involved the police and he confessed to the crime. He was detained, yet all his parents did was to visit him with food without seeking a way to pay me back.

I was advised by the police to take the case to court, which I did and he was remanded pending his judgment. But now he's been freed.

His family didn't do anything about this case, rather they quickly ran around to get him a lawyer.

It's been over 8 months now and I haven't heard from the family. I decided to call off the case because I don't have money to spend on the matter.

The heartbreaking part is that my mother borrowed a huge amount from their women's meeting to help me finance this movement. She's currently battling with health issues and I really don't know what else to do.

The Guy's parents don't talk to me anymore. They believe they've won already and I am really broke right now.

I need an advice on the best way to recover my money and to pay the meeting people my mum borrowed from because they are threatening to seize all our property.

I reported to DPA, but they said they can't do anything since the matter is already in court. The evidence of the transactions are with me."

ISRAEL

"I have been with her for five years and in those five years, not once did she cook when she came to visit.

Even when I come back from work tired and ask her to cook something, she'd suggest snacks instead. Either I cook for myself or go with her suggestion.

To make matters worse, even when I do the cooking, she wouldn't clear the dishes after eating.

My brother's girlfriend lives in the same compound and sometimes cooks and serves me some. My own girlfriend will join me in eating the food and still leave the plates there for someone else to clear.

This behavior of hers annoys my brother so much that he doesn't speak to her.

It is not like she doesn't cook in her own house, she just feels whenever she comes to mine, it's for rest and she cannot be bothered.

I had discussed this with her several times, but she doesn't want to change. Over time, the behavior began to irritate and annoy me and maybe that contributed to my falling out of love with her.My friends advised that I tell her, so we can go our separate ways, but I couldn't bring myself to do it.

While I was still thinking of how to break up with her without hurting her, she visited and told me she'd be getting married to someone her family had arranged for her. Ordinarily, I would have been hurt that she was making such plans while in a relationship with me, but I was happy that she has made my work easy.

I pretended to be offended but was rejoicing inwardly.I honestly pray she doesn't take this attitude to her husband's house because I doubt if anyone will condone it the way I did all these years. "

BUKOLA

"Sometimes I ask myself if God really exists. I have not had an easy life since I was born. My mum told me I came out with legs and I had some complications, but I survived.

From childhood, I have been struggling in one way or the other to meet my needs. Early last year, I fell in love with one man. He was doing everything right which made me feel he was the perfect person for me. He said he'd like to marry me, which I accepted.

He actually wanted to come to my house this December. I did not know what stopped him, but I did not take it too seriously.

Since early February when I told him I was pregnant, he has not called or ask after me or the baby. At first I wanted to do something to myself because I kept asking myself why people bring pain into my life.

God has been faithful for holding me till this point because by now I would have been a dead person. I have made several attempts to remove the baby, but later I decided to keep it. This baby is the only reason I am giving myself a second chance to live again.

I told my mum I don't think I'd want to have anything to do with any man in my life. she kept saying I'd still see a good man to settle down with. I know my decision hurts her a lot but I have made up my mind already.

A man who claimed to love me and all of a sudden, turned his back on me . I really don't know the meaning of happiness right now. The depression I am passing through is something else.

I will give birth next month by God's grace. Whenever I sit down, I only ask God for one thing, if I enter that labor room he should give me another chance to live. I know people will drag me, people will talk about me, people will troll me badly. But if I could overcome the condemnation from relatives, I can withstand them all. "

BARISO

"I'm a depressed woman. I got married a bit late. At 31 years of age. I had to wait for like 2 years to have a child and it was through CS.After 10 months, my boy died. He died in March.

As if that wasn't enough, the same month, my mother stood in as a surety for a neighbor that had a court case involving 2.8 million naira and he eloped. My mother was to provide for him or pay half of the money.

Before the court hearing date, the judge put my mother and the second surety in prison. My mother was there for more than a month. I almost died in the process because I was mourning my baby and at the same time trying to secure my mom's freedom.

I was 18 before my mom had my younger ones, so I am more or less alone because my siblings are also my responsibility since our dad is late. They are like my kids.

I was able to raise 300k with the help of my husband and was given 2 months to provide the eloped man or provide the balance of half of the money.

My mom developed high blood pressure in the process. She was hospitalized during the court hearing, so the court added another one month which is in 2 weeks time to provide the man or the balance of million naira which I don't have any hope of raising.

I'm afraid that my mom might go back to prison if God doesn't come to my aid. I'm so stressed. I'm beginning to give up. I see myself as a failure. "

CHISOM

"This is just a reminder that prayer works. Two weeks ago my kid sister was kidnapped by ritualists. She boarded a keke heading to Madalla, Suleja, Niger state. She lost consciousness and woke up in a room.

It was dark because she was blindfolded. All she could hear was weeping voices, mostly female voices. She said she could sense people leaving the room but none came back.

No one could sleep at home because it was so unusual for her to stay out late.

My mom broke down, started praying and we joined her.

When it got to my sister's turn, they took her inside and removed the blindfold. What she saw made her vomit. She started crying and begging for her life.

As soon as they finished their incantations, the Baba screamed and asked why they brought this kind of person here. He said they should take her back to wherever they brought her from. He said they wouldn't use her because she's a twin and someone followed her there. That if they must use her, then they must use the second person.

When they took her out, the guys decided to go sell her since they couldn't use her. One of them argued and said they should let her go like Baba said that the girl was trouble.

They left her somewhere in Wuye Abuja. People saw her and took her to a hospital. The hospital contacted us through my mom's number. God is wonderful!!! "

AMINA
Part 1

"We're tired and shattered at this point.

It all started on the 24th of June when my mom went for bilateral knee replacement surgery in a private hospital.

Before now, she has had arthritis for over 10 years, which started bending her legs to the point she couldn't walk a long distance again. Standing up looked like the legs would break from the knee.

We had been saving up for this surgery for the past one year when we were told that she needed to go for a knee replacement because her knee joints were both damaged.A private hospital was recommended to us by the HOD, Orthopedic (FETHI) since their hospital doesn't do the surgery.

At the private hospital, my mum had to undergo different tests and diagnosis to confirm she's fit for the surgery and all was good.

On the 25th of June, the surgery was carried out and after a few hours, I noticed that the right leg was cold. I called the doctors. They came and conducted a doppler test which showed there was less blood flow on the limbs.

The next day, she was taken to where she did a CT Scan and this indicated thrombosis on the thigh as a result of the surgery.

At the hospital, we were asking for ways to correct the leg so they can have a pulse again, but they kept saying it'd pick up with time. That there was no need to fear. But after some days the foot was still cold.

Two weeks after the surgery, she was managing to stand and move around in the room. She was using a walker, until she had a dislocation on the left leg.

Meanwhile, the right foot gradually started changing color from the toes because it was still cold. Little did we know it was dry Gangrene that was setting in due to no blood flow. But each time we complained, the doctors kept telling us that we shouldn't be worried that it's nothing."

Part 2

"At 3 weeks when there was no improvement, they gave my mum Streptokinase fluid behind our back to help remove the clothing. However, we were able to notice it because while she was in the fluid, she started bleeding from the anus and surgery sites. She bled for 3 days and within those 3 days, she was given 9 pints of blood to help boost her blood level.

After the incident, they now transferred us out of the hospital with the dry Gangrene that was fast eating up the right leg and a dislocated left leg.

Currently, we're in OAU and we've been spending a whole lot of money. The right leg was later amputated and the left is still unstable. Though it's placed on a backslab to stabilize it for the mean time till when the leg would be operated on again to fix it.

We're asking for a refund of money or even compensation from the 4.5million Naira we paid at the private hospital so we can continue with my mum's treatment, but they don't want to.

They messed up my mum's health and toyed with her even after assuring us she'd walk home 3 weeks after the surgery. Instead, she got worse in addition to the pains she has been going through at 63 years, which at a point affected her mental health.

The thought of being left with one leg which she still cannot move in the bed with is compounding the issue. She's just devastated. She's been bedridden for 2 months with pressure sores. The worst is that she doesn't know when she'll get out of bed.

Is it a crime to ask for a refund to treat the mess they created in my mum's life?

We've currently exhausted all our finances and are still owing because of their greedy and selfish desires.".

FLORENCE

"It hasn't been up to a year since I started living in Abuja. Ever since I came here, the advice I keep hearing is to be beware of Abuja men.

Even my pastor had one time made a reference to it by saying that most Abuja men are nothing but just packaging. That ladies should be careful because some of them are married but will disguise as single men just to leech on a lady.

He went on to say some have cars even when they do not have houses to sleep in.

When he was saying this, I never knew I was going to meet one soon.

Some weeks ago, I booked a ride with a friend. What immediately struck me about the driver was his polished looks and manners. He was very professional and didn't behave like some drivers who would pitch into your discussion uninvited. I decided I was going to give him a good recommendation but by the time the ride ended, I had gotten distracted and forgotten about it.

Later at home when I remembered, I decided to send him a text commending him. That was the beginning of a casual friendship and we would chat on Whatsapp once in a while. He told me he was working for a construction firm but he was running the car hailing service to augment his income.

A few weeks later, he told me he was sick and while he was still trying to recover, he was involved in an accident that damaged his car. For two days, he had to suspend rides to fix the car. Just after he got it fixed, he was held by the Task force for wrongful parking and he had to pay to get his car out.

At the end of all these stories about his misfortunes, he sent me a text asking for a loan of 5000 naira just so he can get fuel to work over the weekend to make some money. He promised to pay back by Sunday.

I was skeptical about giving him the money because I didn't know him so well, but I felt sorry for him for all the troubles he had been through.

Sunday came and passed and his excuse for not refunding was that it had rained all weekend and he was unable to work, but he would refund me regardless.

After then, he stopped picking my calls and responding to my messages and rarely came online.

Sometimes I think maybe something bad has happened to him but with all the stories I've heard, I can't help believing he is fine and just wanted to take money from me.

I feel bad though because I genuinely felt sorry for him and to think he had to behave this way for an amount that small? It just goes to show the truth in what they say about Abuja men."

AMANDA

"I met my husband in 2011 when I was still in secondary school, SS 2. He was a part-time teacher in my school.

At first, I had no intention of being his girlfriend or dating him. He was just a random teacher in my school, but there was something different about him— he was kind, compassionate, and loving. He enjoyed taking care of the students that came around him. Oftentimes, he'd buy clothes and books for those who didn't have.

He encouraged students and he was the students' best teacher and friend. I wasn't the gum body type, so I didn't move that close to him when all the students were flocking around him.

I told my then classmates that whoever would get married to him would surely enjoy it because he's such a caring person.

After some time, I started talking to him and we started getting closer in SS3. Later, we started dating in SS3.

Then he resigned from my school because he wanted to avoid a situation whereby it'd look like he's dating his student.

He started teaching in another school, but we continued dating. He took care of everything that concerned me; clothes, hair, and schooling without asking for anything in return —without bothering me. He encouraged me in my studies.

After I graduated from secondary school, we continued dating. Five years into the relationship, he met my parents and we introduced ourselves. Afterwards, we started planning for our wedding.

Along the line, he lost his mum. Burial ceremonies are always expensive, especially for a first born. He's the first son and almost all expenses then were on him.

So, our wedding was postponed. He used most of the money he had to finance the burial. We kept going. He was such a nice person.

I gained admission into the university. He practically took care of paying for my schooling and everything. In 2019, we did our traditional wedding and also our white wedding.

During the five years of the relationship, the only quarrel we had was when I saw a text message from a lady on his phone. They were chatting. I asked him who she was. He kept saying they were just friends, that she was like his sister. I asked why the person was calling him "baby, honey" if she was like a sister to him.

I reported him to his sisters. They cautioned him, called him to order, and he stopped. That was the only quarrel we ever had since the five years of the relationship after the introduction.

In 2020, I had my first baby. It was 4 months after the wedding. A month ago, I had my second baby. Since then, this marriage has been blissful and peaceful. He does not trouble me . He is the best man ever."

NENYE

"I had my first child through IVF. During one of the hospital visits, it was discovered that one of the babies was already dead. The doctor said removing the dead baby would affect the other one and that since it was already close to my EDD, I should continue carrying them.

When it was time for delivery, an operation was carried. While I buried one child, I went home with one.We were happy that at least one survived but that was when my problems started. I started experiencing different complications.

For two years, I was going from hospital to hospital and no one could figure out what the problem was.

Eventually, one of the new hospitals I visited conducted a scan and it was discovered that the dead child was not properly taken out. Since the problem was discovered, it was easy to get a solution and after another operation and treatment for a while, I got myself back.

Because of the trauma of those years, I didn't think of having another child. For me, the one we had was enough. Unfortunately, my husband thought otherwise. He'd always grumble about how the house was empty with just one child.

When his grumbling increased, I became worried that he might go look for a child elsewhere. I suggested surrogacy and he said I should do what I want but shouldn't expect him to contribute a penny to it.

I made all the arrangements and bore the financial burden alone. I borrowed, did different businesses in addition to my job just to meet up. Luckily for us, the surrogacy went well and we had another child.

My husband who had refused to contribute is now the one gushing over the child. His attitude has changed and he is now very happy. Though I feel sad about how he behaved towards me then, I am happy that we have two children now and for that my home is happier. "

IMMA

"I got married in 2019, but the marriage was not a happy one. My husband turned me into a slave;beating me whenever and wherever he wanted. He'd throw me out of the house and travel, not caring about my safety. Even at night, he'd still throw me out and I'd stay outside till morning.

One fateful day, he locked me up after beating me and wanted to use hot iron on me, but I was able to escape. When he was not around, I came back to pack my things, went back to my family and told them all I had been going through.

My father invited them to discuss the issue, but he refused. After much pleading, he finally came and his response was that he has married and paid my bride price, so whenever I get tired of staying in the village, I can rejoin him in the city.

My people then decided that they wouldn't leave me to die in the name of marriage. They sent a message to him to come take back the bride price he paid. He refused to come until my father died 3 months later.

After my father's burial, he came with a list of what he claimed he did which amounted to about 600,000 thousand naira. On the list were chairs, spoons, disposable plates and other things he had bought for the marriage. My family told him that he's only entitled to the bride price, but he insisted that things must be done his way.Since then, he increases the amount every month.

Last month, he called to inform us that the amount is now one million , three hundred thousand naira and by the end of this year, it'd go higher.

At this point, I am confused and do not know what to do. I am 26 years old, my elder brother is 29 and he's still serving his boss. We have no one to help us deal with this issue."

TREASURE

"My mum had a stroke in 2008 and that changed my family's story. She was our pillar. She catered for all of us, my
Dad included.

Things became hard for us and my dad disappeared in 2011. He only calls or comes home whenever he feels things are getting better and disappears again when things start going wrong.

I couldn't further my education after secondary school. I had to stop and take care of my sick mum and two siblings.

In 2016, we decided to relocate to another side of Abuja. As the first child, I was sent to Lagos to work as a maid in 2017, but my mum's sickness didn't allow me to stay long. I had to come back to continue the struggle here. I found out that whenever I go away from my mum, she gets hit by sickness. She had another stroke last December after I decided to change location because of the new job I got.

I'm back now and I'm doing nothing because I lost my job. My younger brother is the one taking care of us for now.

I pray things get better soon and that my mum gets healthier. I don't want to lose her. She has suffered a lot and I'd like her to at least enjoy the fruits of her labor. "

PEACE

Part 1

"I saw the story a lady shared about abstaining from premarital sex. I want to share my story and experience in this journey called LIFE.

I got admission into a higher institution.

I was a virgin then. I finished my first year

with good grades.

The next year, I met a guy. He was living on my street back at home. I met him while I was on holiday. We became friends, exchanged contacts, and we started dating because he asked me to be his girlfriend.

The relationship was affecting my studies because I was always traveling to see him.

I finished my OND and came back home for my one-year IT. That was when we first had sex. He broke my virginity.

A few months later, when I was doing my IT, the manager called me and asked if I was sick, I told her no. She said she's noticing some changes in my body. She asked the last time I saw my period, I told her, she told me to stay behind after work.

She took me to one pharmacy close to the office and they did a pregnancy test. Lo and behold, it came out positive. I was devastated because I never missed my period for once. I was already four months

gone. I cried my eyes because I knew it was over for me.

I called him and told him, he said I should go and abort.I was naive, so I agreed and followed him. He drove me down to one dirty-looking chemist, but luckily for me the man was not around. We waited there till evening.

When the man came back,we went in, sat down and told him why we came. He checked me and said I was already four months gone. He said he could terminate the pregnancy, but he wouldn't do it.

The guy begged the doctor and even increased the money, the man said no, that he wouldn't touch the pregnancy. My guy left me there in anger and sent me a message that I should do whatever I want with the pregnancy.

I went back home and told my mum and my sister. They were disappointed, but

They accepted me with my baggage.

Three weeks later, this guy came to my house,knelt and begged my mum that he was sorry and willing to take responsibility.

I carried the pregnancy till 9 months. Along the line, he got transferred to Lagos, the communication was good and everything was moving smoothly.

I gave birth to a beautiful girl. He asked me to come over to Lagos. I carried my 2 months and went to Lagos. That was when my nightmare started. He was cheating, keeping late nights, abusing me and my late dad, and always threatening to beat me, which he eventually did.

Part 2

"I advised myself, packed my things, and took a night bus back home. When I got home, my family accepted me. I started working and taking care of myself and my child with the help of my family.

3 months later, he called and asked me what my plan was. I told him I would love to go back to school to finish up my course. I went back to school for my HND with support from him and my family.

The week I graduated, he came to my school, took me out, and proposed to me. I said yes to him.We started the wedding preparations, sent out invitation cards, and paid for every single thing for the marriage.

I traveled down to Port Harcourt to put things in order. COVID-19 came and the interstate lockdown happened. He told me he couldn't travel down to PH. I became ill and the marriage was put on hold.

While I was in PH, I found out I was pregnant again. I told him and he said he's not sure he's responsible for it. He said that when I left his house, I was seeing my period. His family stood by him too.

I carried my pregnancy to full term and gave birth to a baby boy.He heard the news and started calling, telling me to bring his children for him. His family joined him to fight for the custody of the children.

This was a man that denied me and the pregnancy and was cheating boldly to my face while I was with him in Lagos. Most times, he'd lie to the ladies that I was his cousin or his maid. Before I left, I advised him about starting a business, but he rebuffed me and my suggestions. A man that would hit me at the slightest provocation.

Thank God I left because I was down with no one to talk to. At times, he'd leave me at

home with the children. The emotional trauma was eating me up. The gossip about me having two children at home without getting married was getting me depressed.

One day I was alone with my children and a voice in my head kept telling me to give up. I almost harmed myself because I was depressed. I felt worthless because my dreams had been cut short.

I encouraged myself again and moved on with life. For 1 year and 8 months, this man did not care if his children were eating or going to school.

I got a front desk job,worked for 3 months, went to school, finished my clearance and started waiting for service.

Since he heard I got a job, he never cared about sending money. Each time i asked him for money, he'd tell me he didn't chase me out of his house. That since I grew wings to leave his house with his children,I should carter for them.

Well God has been amazing to me. I Thank God for the love and support of my family. My girl is 6 years old and my son is 2 years old. I am 27, still keeping hope alive,because I know I have a great life ahead of me.

As for him, I've lost count of the different numbers he calls with to apologize. He said he's now ready to be responsible and wants his family. But as for me, I've chosen to be responsible now. I thank God I survived all the trauma."

CHARITY

"Sometimes I wonder if my mother is actually my biological mother or she adopted me. I have 2 kids and though we live in the same town, my mother has never stayed up to a month in my house. It didn't matter if I have not fully recovered from delivery. She will stay for just two weeks at most and leave, then visit once in a while but not to spend the night.

The one that shocked me the most was when I gave birth to my third child who I lost eventually. I had a very difficult pregnancy. Though my mother knew what I was passing through, she never came to see me. Even when I requested for my sister to come stay with me for a while, she wouldn't let the girl rest. My sister stayed for three days and my mother started asking her to return home. It's not like there are no other people in the house supporting her.

When my challenges got worse, I had to go in for a Cesarean Operation at the 7th month.Because of the complications, I was bedridden for close to a month. During that period, I had expected my sister to go take care of my other two kids, but she didn't. My mother too didn't think of asking her to come.

My husband would have been able to cope alone, but he still had a business to run so we could foot the growing medical bills. If not for a good neighbor, I don't know what would have happened to my children that period.

I got discharged and went back to the house, while my baby remained in the hospital. I was still recovering, yet I did the chores myself even with my mother around. It's not like she is old and weak. She is young and strong, but she is more concerned about herself and her business than whatever I was passing through.

The day my child died, my mother had just come in the previous day and was planning to stay a while. Not long after we got the news and I had managed to stop crying, my mother said she was leaving. I was speechless but too tired and weak to confront her at that point.

I have reported her to my dad several times. I have also spoken to her myself, but she sees nothing wrong in her attitude. I am well and strong now and I'm trying to let that incident go. I am also praying that nothing happens that will leave me or my children at her mercy again."

TREASURE

"I thought that by the age of 25, I'd be married with kids, but it never happened the way I envisioned it.

Heartbreak has become a regular occurrence in my life to the extent that I have started thinking that I'm the one with a bad character.

However, all the men that have left me to marry someone else always come back to ask me for forgiveness. They usually say that leaving me was the biggest mistake of their lives. So, why then did they leave?

I went into prayers knowing that there is more to this than meets the eye. I'm still hoping that one day, God will hear me and grant my heart desires. To be honest, this

loneliness is really getting to me. "

LIZZY

"I am from Delta state and I was born and bred in Benin but currently based in Istanbul Turkey.

10 years ago, I got pregnant when I was in the 100 level in the University. When I told the person responsible, he denied it and later gave me money to terminate it. When I refused to, he got furious and left me to my fate.

My mom found out when it was already 8 months. She got the number of the guy and called him, but he denied responsibility again. It was later decided that I should terminate it to prevent my dad from finding out.

My mum had thought I was lying when I told her I was 8 months gone because I didn't have a big tummy. I traveled to get the abortion but after checking me, the doctor refused to go ahead with it.

We were introduced to a lady who said she could do it by injecting me so I could have a stillbirth. We agreed and went ahead with it. As God would have it, my baby came out alive.

I informed the father of my child and he warned me not to call him again. The lady offered to take care of the child till we were ready to take him. She reached an agreement with my mom.

My mom and brother engaged the father of my child again and threatened to get him arrested if he refused to take responsibility. That was when he finally accepted and we took him to see the child.

Over time, the lady's attitude towards me changed. She would ignore my calls and even when she picked, she'd act cold.

We decided to go take my child, but the lady chased us out. Eventually, my Dad got to know about the child. To my greatest surprise, he wasn't angry and even went to see him. They agreed my child would continue staying with the lady while he would take care of his upkeep. My opinion wasn't needed. I was only 19 then and still in school.

In the long run, I abandoned the program and traveled out of the country. In my first year abroad, I sent money to my family to take back my son because he was already 3 years old. Little did I know the father of my child had agreed with the lady not to release the child to my family. He sent me a message saying the condition for me to have my child was to marry him otherwise, my child would remain with the lady till he turns 18.

I became depressed and developed hypertension. While trying to make peace so I can get my son, I was arrested for lack of papers and deported. I came back to Nigeria with nothing.

My Dad has tried several times to have a meeting with all the parties involved, but my child's father always comes up with an excuse. He says because I refused to marry him, our child would continue to stay with the woman or his brother rather than with me. I do not know why he has decided to punish me this way especially since he is already married.

I have been patient all these years and my son is 9 years old now and still with this lady. I know I have made mistakes in the past and if I could go back to correct them, I would. I just want my son back because he deserves a better life. I need help and advice on how best to go about this."

ONYINYE

"Some men name their children after their women and side chicks so as to keep remembering the person.

In 1991, my father brought a second wife by name Emelda which happens to be the English name he gave me. That day, he asked my mum to go and make her hair so that we would have a visitor.

Later in the day, the woman came. I call her a woman because she was older than my mum. After the introduction, my father left them to discuss. My innocent mother asked what reason my dad gave her before bringing her in as a second wife. She responded that it's because my mom had only a boy.

My mum was still very young then, and it was still possible for her to give birth to more kids. We were three girls and a boy, but my dad wanted more boys desperately. Hence, he wanted to take another wife— someone much older than my mum.

Even though she was still very young in 1991, my dad still wanted to bring in another wife. Thank God the marriage did not hold. Who would have known our fate now?

My mum later gave birth to more kids.

Now my mum has three boys and five girls(we lost one of the girls).

She gave birth to our son in 2004 at age 39. Our last born being her 9th child.

I am grateful to God that all my mum's daughters are making her proud. Before my dad died, he was also grateful for his girls, but death could not allow him to enjoy more.

He left with the little he enjoyed from his girls."

EMELDA

"I will be 34 in October. I think I'm cursed. I have no job, no boyfriend or suitor. I've been to different churches and I have visited different prophets and even an Alfa. I've gone to the river for spiritual husband settlement but nothing is working.

I'm a very beautiful and determined young woman, but when men see me they say my husband is lucky and show no further interest.

The worst part is that the Alfa I went to wanted to sleep with me after I told him my case. The same happened with the prophet and the babalawo.

My parents are dead and it was revealed at one of the places I went to that my dad's sister is a witch.

At this point, I am tired. I have prayed and fasted, but I think God has forsaken me. Everyone that wants to give me a job will demand for sex first. I'm beginning to think I might as well do it for the money since nothing else is working. I know it's not the best decision, but I'm yet to get a better advice and I really need one right now. "

GODWIN

It hurt, left me broken, changed my attitude, and made me bitter. It was a traumatic experience.

My roommate broke my phone because of a little misunderstanding between us. My phone was my everything. Since ASUU strike started, I have been using my phone to create content, write blog posts,manage pages, and also do other online jobs to get paid.

As a student, I went hungry on some nights just to save to buy the phone. I bought it for 95,000 naira. I went for that grade because of the kind of jobs I was getting.

I was using it to get jobs that were sustaining me. He knew this. Sometimes it's the money I made from working for people that we fed on. Yet, he chose to break my phone.

We had a little misunderstanding and he threatened to break my phone. When the argument became heated, he went to where I plugged the phone, unplugged, and smashed it beyond repair. He knows how important my phone is to me, not just me, but us. I never expected that from him. Now I will have to use the money I'm saving to buy a laptop to learn coding, to buy another phone.

All that kept coming to my mind at that point was how to revenge and fight back.

I noticed that the more I tried, the more broken and damaged I became. It was really a hard time for me. I was going through a lot of pain and I was losing myself.

At some point, I couldn't fight it anymore. All I wanted at that time was to get myself back. I wanted my normal life back but with all the bitterness and quest for revenge that had built up in me,I couldn't. I kept failing.

My last option was to forgive and let go of everything. It was really hard, but I encouraged myself to do it. I forgave and let go of everything that caused me pain.

I let go of that pain,let go of the anger and hatred. I pray that God provides for me."

YUSUF

"My mother was still in the mortuary when my younger sister died. She had gone out in the evening to get something from a nearby market. When she didn't come back after a long time, my brother called her, but her line was switched off.

He went searching for her in places he felt she might have gone, but she wasn't found. I was informed the next morning and I quickly went over to the family house.

We went to make an entry at the police station and the police assured us they would find her.

Days later, her body was found in a refuse dump not too far from our house. We were devastated. After the police were done with their investigations, they let us bury her. We eventually buried our mother too and moved on.

I believe that incident took a heavy toll on my father because his health just deteriorated from there. He has retired to the village and I go to see him at least two weekends in a month.

Recently, I heard that my brother, who now lives in another town, got into a fight and was arrested. We were still trying to get the full information, so we can follow up properly when I got a call that he's dead. He had always been hotheaded. I warned him that if he continued that way, he won't end up well and now he's dead.

In as much as it pains me to lose him, I cannot kill myself over him. What worries me now is how to break the news to my father because he may not survive it."

STANLEY

"I live abroad and I have plans of getting married this year. By God's grace, I am financially stable. My foreign passport is visa free to 185 countries in the world.

Two of my friends have advised me several times to have kids and forget about marriage because women of this generation do not have good character, but I have refused to listen to them.

I met this lady on Facebook. She is in Nursing school in the East and will graduate in November. She will be 25 years old in November while I will be 40 years old in September. I told her I'd be coming home for Christmas. I will also organize a remembrance party for my late parents and brother, and open my house this Christmas.

She asked me my age and when I told her, she said I was too old for her. I tried convincing her that age is just a number and besides, older men are more caring in marriage.

I have been assisting her with money to feed in school even though I have not met her in person, but I've seen her through video calls.

I am beginning to think that what my friends told me is the reality and it would be best to follow their advice. I may just have kids and when they're old enough, I'll bring them over to join me if I am still living abroad.

I get discouraged by the day, but I will wait till the end of the year to make a decision. "

CHIDIEBERE
"My brother had served his boss for 7 years and was due for settlement, but his boss kept telling him to be patient.

In the 8th year, my brother could not wait any longer as nothing much was coming from working for his boss and he needed to start off on his own.

What he had learnt was heavy duty truck driving. His plan was to work for others till he can save up to get his own truck.

He got a place, told his boss, and left. The boss wasn't happy with him, but he couldn't make him stay either. He promised to settle my brother when he has money.

A month after my brother got the job, he returned from a trip one day, parked, returned the keys as usual, and went home.

The next morning, he got to the office to hear that the truck was stolen. He was arrested with two others. Though they eventually released the other two persons, my brother has been in detention since then. He was later moved to the prison and has been there for over two years now.

We do not have money for any case. We have sold everything we have to get a lawyer, but nothing has come out of it. He is in Lagos and I haven't gone there to visit because I can't afford it.

Any money I raise from my business goes to the lawyer.We heard it was his former boss that planned everything to make him a scapegoat, but we cannot prove that.

I just pray that someday, the truth will come out and my brother will be set free.

GIDEON

"I have escaped death countless times,but one of the most tragic experiences was when law enforcement agents almost got me killed in Makurdi, Benue state.

I'm a student of Benue State University. There was a high rate of killings and cult activities in the state.

One day, I came into the state capital late at night, so I went to a roadside spot to get some food. On my way back to the house, I saw a group of policemen buying suya. I had this feeling within me to pay for their suya. After paying, one of them appreciated me and they left.

Unknowingly to me, they were on their way to our street to raid.As I got to the street, I started hearing gunshots.All of a sudden, I heard a very frightening voice behind me.

"Freeze! if you move I will shoot you."

" Place your hand on your head, turn around, and get down on your knees"

I went down on my knees. They came and put handcuffs on me. As that was happening, they arrested four other guys after exchanging bullets with the cult boys.

When they were done with the arrest, they called their head office and gave them a situation report about the arrest and that they were on their way to the station.

We could all hear them through their walkie-talkie when their boss was telling them not to bring us to the station; rather, they should waste us and dump our bodies in River Benue.

They called one of their members and asked us to queue up. We were five in number. I was the 4th person on the line.

Their leader gave the order and they shot the first person and shot the second person.

The third guy on the queue shared the same fate.

When it got to my turn, one of them flashed a light on my face. He recognized that I was the person that paid for their suya. He told their boss and they released me. They shot the 5th guy immediately and I was released. That was how God preserved my life that day."

PRISCA

"I'm a single mother of one. I had two children, a boy and a girl, but the girl is late now and my boy is staying with my uncle. He attends one of the best private schools in my local government and my uncle foots all his bills.

I stay in the capital of my state, Gombe. I met a kind man there who has been a brother, father, husband, and boyfriend. He pays my rent and feeds me.

I'm an NCE holder. If not because of the strike, I would have gone back to get a degree because he gave me some money to apply for part-time studies which I have already done. But because of the ASUU strike, my admission is pending.

This man is the best of all the men I've dated. He makes a lot of sacrifices when it comes to anything that concerns my son and I. He has always wanted me to bring my son to come stay with me, but my uncle's wife doesn't want him to leave.

My worry is that I'd like to get married, but my boyfriend says marriage shouldn't be my problem for now since I already have a child. His plan is to develop the land he bought for me; so I can have my own house, have a thriving business, and a degree before we can get married.

Most times I get agitated that he may not marry me. Maybe he'd provide all these things and end up leaving me. I am not the kind of person that double dates. If not I would have been in another relationship so that when he leaves me, I'd drop my eggs into that other basket.

I need some advice and words of encouragement. Most importantly, I need prayers and good wishes. I love this man very much. He has everything I need in a man and even more. But I am afraid of being jilted as I am 30 years already. "

CHUKS

"When there is an issue between a landlord and tenant, most people will support the tenant. Landlords are always seen as the wicked ones without conscience. That is why I am always careful to avoid any altercation with my tenants.

I have had different tenants with different characters, but none as bad as the young lady I rented out my shop to two years ago.

She took the shop in January 2020. She said it was to be used for her tailoring business. She paid for one year and moved in.

Because I don't live there, I don't know what goes on there. Unfortunately, the pandemic came and lockdown started so my going out to check activities at my properties was also limited.

Months later, I discovered she was living in the shop. It wasn't supposed to be a residential place, but I allowed her considering how everything was turning upside down then. I also got to find out from neighbors that she hardly made any clothes and appeared not to know her trade, and so had no customers. It wasn't my business, so I didn't think much of it.

The following year, her rent became due for renewal and I went to demand for it. She asked for extra time which I gave her.

The extra time turned into months and instead of being apologetic, she started becoming confrontational. She would call me names saying I had no conscience. I saw how bad the last year was and how she didn't make any money from her business.

This went on till the year ended. Meanwhile, in the course of this period, I asked her to move out and forfeit the rent, but she refused.

I wanted to use force to send her packing but knowing how troublesome she was, I decided to do everything legally.

Early this year, I contacted a lawyer and the matter was taken to court. She didn't come to court for one day. In the end I got a judgment against her. The court clerk and police had to follow me to the shop to bring her things out. You should have seen how this lady was fighting everyone. They wanted to go lock her up for contempt of court, but people around pleaded on her behalf.

The case cost me money. I also lost the rent I would have gotten in two years, but I am happy she has finally left. If she were to be humble and nice, maybe I would have given her time to continue her business. But with her bad character, it was best to send her away.

The shop is vacant for now and I will be very careful when selecting the next occupant."

WAHEEB

"We both wanted children, so when there was no sign of pregnancy months into the marriage, I became worried. She was, however, not as worried as I was. I'd ask that we go for a test and she'd insist nothing was wrong with her.

When we eventually did, I went alone to take the result. The doctor told me I was fine while she had an infection that had stayed too long in her system and it has affected her chances of getting pregnant. I was very angry because I assumed she must have known all these years.

We started treatment and she wasn't serious about it. At some point, the doctor recommended IVF. I had to use all my savings and even borrowed to do it. In the end, it failed.

We had to go seek a second opinion. It was this second doctor that suggested we treat the infection completely before trying to have children. Because the doctor was in another state, she decided to relocate there. I didn't object because all I wanted was for her to be fine. Even when she refused to visit me after relocating, I still didn't ask her to return to our base.

Where it got bad was when I started hearing tales about her. She was staying in my cousin's house since my cousin and his family lived in another city. The gateman would call my cousin to complain about how she was coming back late in the night and sometimes drunk.

The worst was when my niece said she saw her in a club. To be sure it was her, my niece approached her and asked her what she was doing there with another man. She had to plead with my niece not to tell me. My niece had expected her to leave after that confrontation, but she didn't. Rather, she still followed the man to a hotel. My niece said she had watched and followed her all through the night so she could be very sure before coming to me.

I have tried talking to her, but she doesn't listen. She will just start crying to make you feel guilty. Even with the treatment she went there for, she hardly visits the hospital for it. I do not know how she can get well and how we can try to have children when we do not make love.

Honestly, I'm tired of the marriage, but I love her and wouldn't want to leave just yet. If we had not dated for long, I would have said she doesn't love me, but we dated for 3 years before we got married and she wasn't like this in the beginning.

Right now, I have decided to let her be. Once I can get a break from work and visit her, I will sit her down and ask her if she still wants to continue or if we should go our separate ways. "

ABDUL

"With the current security situation in the country, the best advice I would give to anyone now is to always be on alert. Avoid going to places that you are not familiar with. Most importantly, avoid staying out late.

My wife and three kids have gone back to the village. Immediately the kids finished their exams,I asked them to get ready so that they would be spending the holidays down there in the village. I'm the only one here now.

The government has to do something fast to protect the lives of the citizens they have sworn to protect because it won't be a good thing if the citizens are left to defend themselves.

Gradually, we are drifting away from that peaceful and united country that we were known for to a failed nation. We can't continue living as if everything is okay. More people need to come out and start speaking the truth to the authorities for things to get better."

EJIRO

"Seeing my brother off at the park to NYSC camp was one of the happiest days of my life. He had told me not to bother, but I insisted. I was overjoyed and my business could wait. It was at night after the day's hustle and I was finally on my bed that I cried. But they were tears of joy. I was remembering everything that happened and how we got here.

After my parents died, I had to stop schooling in my SS1 to hustle so my younger ones could continue. I remember how I'd leave the house very early to join other women at the bush market.

At first, those who didn't know me thought I came with my mother or an older person. It was after they had seen me consistently that they knew I was on my own and the business was mine.

I was young. I had never done any business in my life, but I was willing to learn. I learnt fast and some months down the line, I could afford to pay our rent and avoid the risk of being homeless.

My parents weren't rich, but they at least provided our basic needs. After my mum died, my dad tried to play both roles, but it wasn't long before he too died. The few relatives we had supported us during the burial but after that, nobody asked us how we were going to survive without our parents.

We came back to the city and life continued. Even though I was young, I was old enough to know the situation we were in and that I had to take responsibility for my two siblings.

There was never a time it was easy but I was determined to keep us alive and together. What helped me the most was that my siblings were supportive. Whenever they were on break, they helped with the business. Whatever is in season, I sell but most times, I sell oranges because it hardly goes scarce.

It is from this business I trained my siblings to this level. There were times we thought they would drop out because I couldn't afford their school fees.

Many times, I gave up my own pleasures so they could get their school needs. Many times, I borrowed. So, seeing my brother graduate with good grades and go off to service is something we all thought at the beginning was impossible.

My younger sister is in her final year, but the strike is holding her back. I am just happy that my hard work is paying off and I pray that their education will help them get a better life."

TEGA

Hustling brought me to the south. Though my parents are from the south, we were all born and bred in the north.

After dad lost his job, things became very difficult for us. My siblings and I started looking for ways to support the family. I got an offer to come work for someone and had to move down here. It was during that job I met my daughter's father.

We started dating and I moved in with him. When I got pregnant, we both agreed to keep it. Though he wasn't doing so well financially, he could take care of our basic needs.

After I gave birth, his attitude towards me changed. He still provided it though, especially when it had to do with his daughter. He was a good and loving father and tried his best for her, but it appeared he no longer wanted me. I was ready to endure because of my daughter. I no longer had a job and was fully dependent on him.

I became afraid when he started talking about taking my child away from me . He had relatives abroad who he said would be willing to take the child. Apart from the fact that I wanted to be close to my child, how could anyone think about taking a two year old child abroad? My mind told me something was fishy.

When I told my mother, she said she wouldn't afford to lose her first grandchild. Though she was struggling financially, she raised some money for the transport fare and sent it to me. The day I left, I didn't give him any hint. In fact, I left the house with only a handbag.

When he waited till evening and we weren't back, he called. I told him I had left town to go live with my sister. He cursed and threatened but there was nothing he could do about it.

It's been over a year since I left. I live with my sister and mother and together we are hustling to make things better. The father of my child has not sent a penny to us since we left. He calls once in a while and I let him talk to his daughter."

PRISCA

"I am in a very confused and bitter state right now. I was in a relationship with a guy in January this year and now, I'm over 5 months pregnant with his child. He has not been able to do anything financially and it doesn't seem like he's going to do anything. All he does is give excuses.

The most hurtful part is that while in the relationship, he always forced himself on me whenever he felt like having sex and when he's done, he'd ask for forgiveness and promise never to do it again.

I know it was entirely my fault for condoning it all these while. I just can't forgive myself or get over the fact that my life is ruined by his selfishness and he's not making things easier for me. I've been the one taking care of my medical bills and I'm tired.

I've been taken advantage of and sexually abused several times all through my life and I can't do anything about it. My family and everyone are overlooking the fact that he raped me all because I failed to say anything from the onset and let it happen severally.

Honestly, I wish I could just forget about it and try to move on, but I can't. I feel like I am going insane each passing day with the thoughts of nothing being done to him and my life all messed up due to his selfish acts.

Right now, I do not know what to do or how I'll come out of this situation alive and sane. I never wanted to keep this pregnancy but just couldn't go through with aborting it and now I feel like I made a mistake."

IJEOMA

"I met this guy in 2019 and we started dating in 2020. Same year, I got pregnant with him and he said I should keep it, but due to circumstances surrounding my final year studies, we later agreed to terminate it.

In 2021, I got pregnant again but because I had earlier treated an infection and was afraid of infertility, I decided not to abort any pregnancy again.

When I told him about the pregnancy, he got angry and denied it. He had accused me of double dating because of chats he read on my phone. I had, however, explained and apologized to him and he told me he had forgiven me only for him to use it against me.

After some weeks of being hard and mean, he finally agreed to take responsibility on the condition that we would no longer be dating. He kept to his words and even did more than I expected.

Now, he has come to say he will take the child after 2years. I have never thought of giving birth to someone and getting married to another. Neither have I ever thought that another woman would train my child for me.

I am confused right now as I do not want a situation where I'll be fighting over my child with a man. On one hand, I am praying for things to work out between us. On the other hand, I am wondering if that will ever happen and if it is the right thing to do. "

TOBI
"All my life, I have never benefitted anything from the government. Right from when I was a kid, I have watched my parents pay their taxes and bills diligently without defaulting or looking for shortcuts.

The amazing part of it is that the house we live in was built by my parents from their earnings. They are not civil servants. The water in the house is a borehole which was also provided by parents.

We are four in number. My siblings and I all attended a private school due to the deplorable conditions of the government schools we have around my locality.

I have long lost hope in the country since I was 14 years old. We keep on recycling old sets of corrupt politicians that have held this country hostage even before I was born. But everyday, you will keep on hearing things like: "Be patient, things will get better."

It's not rocket science, things will never get better until we flush out all these old selfish politicians out of our political system. That's the only time things would get better.

The only thing still keeping me here is my service year. Once I'm done with it, I'm traveling out for my MSc and will never return until the country is fixed.

My secondary schoolmates that did their university education abroad are all doing well already and have lots of opportunities that will make their future bright.

The truth most people won't want to hear is that there is no future for any young person in this country. My honest advice is leave this country if you can. This country kills young talents and startups. Once you are not within the political class, nothing for you.

KATE

"When my friends were telling me to focus on myself and leave my brother alone, I thought they didn't mean well for me and my family. Now I've wasted the resources I should have used in making myself better on someone who doesn't value nor appreciate my help.

I have two elder sisters, both married and not struggling financially. Yet, they do not care how their other siblings and their mother are surviving.

From a young age, after our father died, I have had to take care of my mother and brother. Though my mother is engaged in a petty business, she's old and doesn't make much from it.

As our only son, I felt it would be good for my brother to go to the university, so he can have better opportunities. But the boy has refused to be useful.

First time he gained admission, I know how hard I saved and how much I borrowed to pay his fees. Only for him to get himself withdrawn at year two because of underperformance.

A couple of years after that, he did nothing. I encouraged him to get a job at least. Even when I got him one, he would be complaining about the salary and wouldn't go. My plan was for him to go back to school and I was saving for it.

This year, I told him to try again. Luckily, he gained admission. I gave him my ATM card to go pay his fees. To my shock, he emptied my account and disappeared. I just couldn't believe that my own brother I have been struggling for will be this wicked to me.

Rather than talk about the money he stole, my mother is worried about his safety wherever he might be. This act finally brought me to my senses.

Henceforth, it will be just me. I also want a better life for myself and I'll start putting myself first to achieve it. "

SARAH

"We met on Facebook. Immediately he knew I was from his tribe, so he proposed marriage. I am above 35 years and have been anxious to get married. Still, I asked him to slow down, that I would like us to date for a while. He said he didn't want to date and was sure of what he wanted.

Within two months of meeting, we got married. That same period, I had rented a new apartment and opened up my salon. I was previously staying in an open space in the market. He encouraged me to sell off most of my properties in the apartment since I'd be moving in with him. I did and used the money to contribute to our wedding ceremony.

Few months after the marriage, he started taunting me with pregnancy. His mother would also call to harass me.

Before marriage, the church had asked to do a fertility test. He refused but since we did other tests, the church didn't insist on it.

When he started taunting me, I told him we should go run the test to know if something was wrong with either of us. He still refused and said nothing was wrong with him, that I must have destroyed my womb in my early years moving from one man to another. There was no insult I didn't get.

I started looking for solutions. The hospital told me I was okay and I should bring my husband. I also went to churches. Since I knew nothing was wrong with me, I started suspecting the fault was his. I decided to keep a record of his actions and the things he said. I'd record our conversations and even his mother's calls taunting me.

From my snooping around, I found out he was cheating. I kept all these to myself and kept disturbing him to go for a test. He finally accepted when I called both families together and told them to beg him.

My fears were confirmed. He didn't have any sperm in his semen. In fact, the problem had been with him for years and he knew. What pained me the most was how he mistreated me even when he knew he was at fault.

I called both families again to play the recordings I had. Immediately the first one started, he grabbed the phone and smashed it on the floor. He didn't know I had also sent them to my sister. But there was no need to get them from her, I was done with the marriage and nobody could make me stay.

He refused me taking any of the gifts we got from the marriage. Even the wrappers given to me, he said it was his people that bought them. I didn't struggle with him over anything but just took my personal belongings and left.

I thank God I still have my shop and with hard work, I will recover the things I lost and get another apartment. If God wants me to still get married, he will bring another man and this time, I'll be more careful."

ARDEBAYO
"Honestly, I'm ashamed of myself. I have failed my kids and wife in every aspect they look up to me as a father. I have anger management issues. It takes a little mistake for me to just pick a quarrel with someone and before you know it, it will lead to a fight. Most of these things happen in front of my kids.

One day I was driving with my kids and while I was trying to take a left turn, there was a vehicle coming from the direction which I wanted to drive into. The driver signaled for me to wait for him to drive out, but I ignored and asked him to wait for me to pass. The driver didn't even respond; he just kept quiet. I got angry immediately and wanted to come down from the car, but my wife asked me not to. I ignored her and came down.

On approaching the vehicle, the driver came down and asked me to go back to my car and reverse so that he can pass. I refused and asked him to reverse for me instead. Next thing I felt on my chin was a heavy punch. Before I could realize what was happening, I was on the ground already and this guy gave me a serious beating.

Thank God for my wife and some passersby that intervened on my behalf. If not, that guy would have killed me. He gave me the beating of my life and not just that, he still got me locked up. While people were pleading with him to calm down, the next thing I saw was a military pick up van and some uniformed men. They came down, saluted him, and took me away.

It was my wife that pleaded with him before I was released. Before then, he sat me down and advised me. He asked me to learn how to put my anger in check and be a responsible husband and father to my family.

After that incident, I became a totally changed person. I'm still trying my best to make it up to my kids and wife because I have really brought them enough shame and disgrace due to my anger issues. Thank God I have finally overcome that. What's left for me now is making up with my family and those I have wronged. "

PRECIOUS
"I am a student and I am currently staying with my elder sister due to the ASUU strike. I usually spend my holidays with her family. I do all the chores in the house. I practically do everything. She does not help with anything at all. Even when I am sick, I will still do the chores because I have no choice.

Before the strike, I told her I wouldn't be coming over to her place unless they can get me a job or enroll me in a fashion school. They agreed. When the strike started, she told me she had gotten a job for me and I immediately traveled down to their place only to find out it was a lie. I was forced to stay back. They make me feel like a nanny and slave. The only time I go out is when I'm going to the market. I don't even have friends.

What I need now is a job or a sponsor for a fashion school because my sister and her husband have refused to sponsor me. Sometimes I feel like running away, commiting suicide, or doing something stupid.

The worst part is that my parents do not like me complaining and have refused to listen to me. They say by complaining, I am disrespecting my sister. The situation has become unbearable for me and I need an advice on what to do."

TITILAYO

"I am in a dilemma. I am in a relationship with a young man. He has met my family officially and plans to come marry me before the end of the year.

There's another man seeking for my hand in marriage. I don't love him. I feel absolutely nothing for him, but two of my pastors said God told them he's my husband.One pastor already said before that he saw me marry the new guy and was regretting it.

Now, I don't know if I should go ahead and marry my boyfriend or leave him for the new suitor. I am so scared of making mistakes.

I want to marry right.What if I marry my boyfriend and regret it? I can't stay a day without talking to him for the past 5yrs of the relationship.He's my business partner. My gossip mate. We literally talk about any and everything.

My question is, has anyone been told by pastors that someone is their husband and they didn't listen? If yes, did you regret your decision?

If I have to go for the new guy,how do I break up with my boyfriend? I can't survive a whole day without talking to him. After the 2nd pastor said the same thing, I decided to reduce the frequency of our phone calls to see if I can break up from there. Just one day of not speaking to him, it was as if the world was falling apart.I never felt the same till we talked.I got a gist and started calling to gist him forgetting I told myself I wanted us to stop talking frequently.

How do I break up with such a man? What if I finally marry him and regret it? What if I marry the new suitor and regret it too?How do I even marry someone I dislike?

Advice me, please. If you are or have been in the same shoes as me, how did you handle it? I don't sleep at night because of overthinking? "

FEEDBACK

I am here to thank you guys a lot. Your advice helped revive my faith.

I did fasting and also midnight prayers.

I wrote their names on pieces of paper. At the end of the fasting each day, I'd ask God to make me pick my husband, so I can pray for him. Each time, I picked my boyfriend,I still told God I needed more convictions.

One day, I told God I needed him to convince me in any way that my boyfriend is his will for me. I was just praying and my phone vibrated. I opened my eyes and it was a text message from my boyfriend which said "My baby, I can't wait to make you my wife "

Maybe it was another conviction or a coincidence, but it has happened like 3 times; I'd be praying and would get up to a text of how blessed he'd be if he finally marries me.

I still said I was going to test the two men. I called both of them and told them that if we'd get married, the wedding would be in my church. My boyfriend laughed and asked if it's church that's going to make him not to marry me and that even if they want him to baptize in the church, he will gladly do so.

The other man said never ,that it's impossible. He asked his mum and she said it's impossible too. I told him it's not possible for me to wed in their church. It led to a quarrel that he even had to ask me to refund the money he had earlier sent for me to get something for him.

He didn't call for 3 days after that. When he finally called, it was to ask if I had changed my mind. When I told him I haven't , he said that the wedding cannot be in my church and he would rather end everything and get someone else.I saw it as God bringing a means to eliminate him from my life and I praise Him for answering my prayers.

My parents are the problem now. They said they prefer the new man because he's from my tribe while my boyfriend is not. My Dad had sworn that it would be over his dead body that I would get married to the new man or bring another person. I thought I was done with my problems only for the devil to now want to use my parents.

My boyfriend initially wanted to come do the traditional rites in October, but when I told him the situation, he decided to move it forward to August. He said he'd be coming with elders from his village and their king, his uncle, so when my parents say he cannot marry me, they'll be able to ask questions

.

The day my parents called and told me I can't marry my guy, I just went inside, got on my knees and started praying. When I opened my Bible, God led me to so many scriptures that gave me relief. My prayer now is for my parents to accept my boyfriend. I really want to marry him. He has 8/10 of the things I need in a husband while the new man only has 2/10. He is only richer than my boyfriend, but I do not care as I am not lazy. My boyfriend and I working together will achieve a lot as we have been doing.

My people, how can I make my parents allow my boyfriend to come with his people? My father already said he'd chase them away if they come. Who had their parents against their marriage initially and how did you handle it?"

AHMED

"When I grow up, I would like to be a responsible father to my children. I will try my best to make sure I'm able to provide their needs and ensure that they get basic education.

My mother is such a hardworking and wonderful woman. She has been the one ensuring that my siblings and I are not out of school. She is also providing our basic needs, unlike my father who has refused to go and look for something to do. He's such a lazy man that can't even provide water for his family. Sometimes he would expect my mother to cook and keep his share while we go hungry, but my mother makes sure that we eat first and leave whatever is left for him.

My father will wake up in the morning, have his bath, and go to one place with his likes to play ludo and board games. Most times I'm ashamed to address him as my father, especially when my schoolmates come around.

My siblings and I help our mother everyday with sales once we come back from school. She has a stand in front of our house. My brother and I carry some of the goods around to sell so that she would make more sales and be able to meet up with our needs.

Sometimes we make sales of up to 10,000 naira daily. All thanks to some of the customers that patronize us. Even when they don't need what we sell, they will just buy to encourage us. We always remember them in our prayers.

My most desired goal in life is for my children to be proud of me. I want to be a hardworking and responsible man that would add value to society.

FUNMI

"I already had two children for a man who until his death only made promises to complete the marriage rites he started after our first child. That child was 7 and the second child was 5 when he died.

I continued living with his family for two more years before finally deciding to leave. It was after I left I started dating again. That was when I met him. I told him about my previous marriage and that I had two children. He said it didn't matter to him. Before long, I was pregnant and he asked me to move in with him.

That was when I should have taken my leave of the relationship or just continued dating him from where I was. But back then, I was weak and afraid. I wasn't thinking straight.

I moved in with him and he started misbehaving. This man would wake up in the morning and decide it was a day for abusing me. He'd just take a seat and start raining curses on me and my family.

He'd insult me in public at the slightest provocation. I endured and even had another child for him.

I stopped talking about marriage because it'd only attract insults. The funny thing is, he didn't have much and I was contributing a lot from my petty business. Yet this man would not stop telling me how useless I was and that no man would pay a dime on my head because I was already wasted with four children.

The day I told myself it was enough, nobody believed it. I didn't give him any hint. I had sent my children away for the holidays, so it was easy for me to leave. We woke up as usual and after he went out, I made arrangements for a vehicle and moved everything I had. I can only imagine the shock he must have felt when he returned.

He first came threatening me to return, then he switched to insults, and now he is begging. It has finally dawned on him that I am done. It's been over 8 months. He is still begging, but I am 100% sure I am not going back. I am also done with men. I will use what is left of my life to take care of my children."

WOLE

"My marriage was barely two months old when my mother called to tell me a lady brought a child to the house saying it's mine. She said she had no doubts because the child looked like me. I told her I couldn't travel home that period but that I'd like to speak with the lady.

It turned out it was someone I was dating before I got married.We had just started dating when she told me she was traveling and then I didn't hear from her for about two months. Her numbers were not going through and I didn't know her family, so there was nobody to contact. The only friend that knew her told me she was fine and would relay my messages.

When she called me two months later, it was to tell me she was pregnant. I told her to return, so we can put our heads together and plan. I told her to keep the baby as I was ready to foot whatever responsibilities that would come with it. She accepted and then disappeared again. I neither saw nor heard from her for another two months.

Then she would call once in a while to demand for money and I'd always give her. I couldn't reach her, nor did I see her all through her pregnancy. I moved on with my life and finally got married and then she disappeared.

After my mother's call, I was worried, especially about how my wife would react. For days, I couldn't look her in the face and she kept pushing to know what was wrong.

Some months later, we traveled to my place for an event. While we were there, I started making inquiries on how to reach her. I finally got an address in Lagos.

I went there and fortunately found her. She couldn't come up with a reasonable excuse on why she has been going on and off. I told her we should go for a test but she refused. She said if I won't take her word for it and believe her, then I should forget about it. I saw the child too and contrary to what my mother said, I didn't see any resemblance.

While I was there, the man she is currently with came and the son ran to him calling him daddy. She introduced me as a friend and shortly after, I left. We couldn't continue the discussion in the man's presence.

When I returned, I told my wife about it. She was not happy, but there's nothing we can do about it. I really wish to know if the child is mine, so I can do what is right. But when the mother is not being truthful to me or the current man, I get confused. I have decided to let her be and until she agrees to a test, I will not be responding to any demands from her

ASHLEY

"My husband never wanted anybody to live with us. His work takes him off town for months, leaving my daughter and I alone in the house.

My business requires me to go out only once in a while, so most times, I'd be home and bored. Even in the evenings when I'll need someone to talk to, it will still be just me and my daughter.

When my cousin started asking to come live with me, I had to beg my husband before he accepted. She was yet to gain admission and was always home too like me. I noticed she started moving around with some boys in the estate.

Before long, she started dating one of them. I knew one of my older male friends would love to date her and since she needed the financial assistance that would come with the relationship, I told her about the man. To me, it was better than dating the small boy that would do her no good. Her family won't be able to afford her tertiary education and my husband and I could only support to the best of our abilities.

I introduced her to the man and they started dating. The only condition I gave was for her not to sleep over at his place. Because the man is my friend, we sometimes went to his house together. One time, he had to beg us to sleep over. He had a big house and got his housekeepers to prepare a room for me and my child while my cousin joined him.

In a short while, I could see the changes in her life. She started looking better and buying good clothes and hair. I never for once asked her how much she was getting or did I demand to get any from her. I only advised her to save so she can have something for school .

Then, my husband's younger sister came to join us. The two of them became close friends and often went out together. I never thought anything bad about their friendship since it was better for everyone to live in peace. Little did I know that two of them had other plans.

It happened that we had a burial to attend in my village. We all traveled home including my husband. My husband called my family for a meeting and while everyone was seated, he called out to my cousin and his younger sister to narrate what had been happening.

Right before me, my cousin said I introduced her to a man and I've been taking the money the man was giving her and only gave her a little from it. In other words, I was pimping her to men. My sister-in-law quickly corroborated the story. I was dumbfounded.

My father spoke up first and asked if it was true. That was the biggest shock of my life. What will I say? I just stood there with tears running down my eyes. It was when my husband said I shouldn't return to his house that I fell down begging.

I looked at my sister-in-law and just had to expose the secret I thought I could keep for her.Right there too, I told my husband how his mother had called me to beg that she come stay in my house from where she would go terminate a pregnancy and after she healed, she can return home. I asked my husband if he knew that about his mother and sister. He was shocked. She herself couldn't deny it. He stormed out and left me there on the floor crying and begging.

I eventually went back to my house the following week after my husband had gone back to work. With the intervention of my family and friends, we reconciled.

As for my cousin and my sister-in-law, they couldn't return to my house. I had to send their personal effects to them. They have called my husband to beg to return, but he tells them to come beg me instead as I'd be the one to live in the house with them. Of course, they cannot come to me. Not after what they did and tried to break my marriage.

Honestly, I regret my actions. I thought I was helping a young girl that was not even naive in the first place. I didn't know I was shooting myself in the foot. "

EMMANUEL

"I had always hated the creek boys as we called them. To me, they were no different from those in the North who were killing people indiscriminately. Though the creek boys rarely killed their victims, there have been cases where their kidnapped victims died in their hands. There have also been gun fights between them and the military. I never knew a day would come when I'd become their victim and get to see things from their perspective.

We had set out on a business trip that fateful morning. Me, my boss, and two naval escorts. It was supposed to be a 5-hour boat ride. We had done about 3 hours and were deep in the mangrove when suddenly, this other boat appeared from a curve with gunfire blazing. Before the naval officers could react, our boat was hit, and I found myself struggling to stay inside. In a twinkle of an eye, two of them were inside our boat. They told us to cooperate so nobody would be hurt. We were blindfolded before we continued the journey. The next place I found myself was in a bit of clearing in the mangrove. They had made a makeshift tent. That was to be our home for the next five days.

Surprisingly, they were nice to us. Not once did they hit us. I even got close to a couple of them and started asking them questions. They told me about the degradation in their lands. The fact that they see the oil and the money it brings to the country yet they themselves get nothing. Not even pipe borne water and electricity. While we were there, getting food and water took at least two days and rather than starve us, they gave us whatever was left and waited till the next supply came. They even gave up their mosquito nets for us. Listening to their stories made me very sad. Though I do not support the path they chose, I understood why. If they had better options, maybe they wouldn't go this way. I even asked for their number since I knew they wouldn't harm us but they refused to give.

It was on the 5th day they took us out and when we got to a particular location, left us and returned. Soon, we saw a naval boat that came to take us out of the place. I got to know later that the Navy had threatened fire and brimstone and they decided to let us go to avoid further trouble.

Sometimes I think about those young men and what has become of them. If they had agreed to give me a number, maybe I would have been able to support them and get them away from that place and that life."

ABDULLAHI

"Most times in life we don't usually get what we wish for. While growing up, I had a comfortable life. My father was a civil servant. We attended a private school unlike most of our friends that their parents couldn't afford to send them to private schools.

Unfortunately, I lost my dad in Primary 4 and shortly after, I lost my mum, leaving only my 3 siblings and I. Things became really hard for us that we could barely feed. My father's younger brother took us in and we lived with him until I was 15 years old.

I had to leave the house to go and look for a means of survival for my siblings and I. I have done several jobs and learnt several skills, but finally I settled for sewing. I buy empty sacks, sew them, and sell to traders which they use in sampling and covering their goods.

From this trade, I have been able to send my siblings back to school and also provide all their needs. I would be the happiest man to see my siblings graduate from the university. Since I couldn't achieve that, I would like to see them achieve it. It's my responsibility as their elder brother to make sure my dreams and theirs come through."

BOSE

"I grew up without a father. Whenever I visited my friends' houses and saw they had father, mother and siblings, i'd be wondering why it was different in my own house. It was always just my mother and I. Because I found the house lonely most times, I'd follow a friend home after school and stay there till evening.

The first time I asked my mum why it was just the two of us, she got angry and asked if she wasn't trying hard enough for me. Her reaction told me it wasn't something she liked talking about.

As I grew older and got into secondary school, I became bolder with my questions. It was after my junior secondary exams she finally answered them. She was an only child and an orphan. When she got pregnant while in secondary school, the uncle she was living with chased her out. She ran to her boyfriend, my father, but he denied her and also sent her away. She had to struggle her way through life and left our state to this place to start life afresh.

I felt very bad for her and could only imagine the trauma she had gone through. There and then, I decided I was going to be a better man than my father was. I may not be perfect, but I know I'm trying. I have one of the best relationships with my child. On weekends when I don't go to work, I do everything for her from bathing to feeding and if I have to go get something, I also go with her. Apart from giving my wife time to rest, it's also a bonding time for my daughter and I. God willing, I will give her all the emotional support I never had and make sure she never gets to feel the neglect I felt as a child."

ISMEAL

At first, the Boko Haram were giving money to join them. They would even give to your family and promise you more. Most families started pushing their sons to join them. My family never supported what was going on and so there was no talk of me joining. Then they started forcing people to join. If you refuse, they'd beat you and still take you away with them. That was when my family started looking for ways for me to leave.

When someone from the city came and said he needed boys to work with him, my family quickly made the arrangement for me to go with him. This was not what I had anticipated, but it's still better than joining people to fight and end up dying in the process. I still hear what happens and also hear from my family once in a while. It's been two years since I came here and I haven't gone home. I miss home, but my family has not asked me to return yet. They too are not stable. They are always running from one place to another. I am praying for the day all these will end so I can be reunited with my family."

AMINA

"This is our seven years of marriage without a child. At the beginning, the doctors said nothing was wrong with us. While he was calm about it, I couldn't help worrying. I am the one people always ask questions and gossip about. So even after he stopped following me to different places for a solution, I continued. That was when I discovered I had a fibroid. They said it's not very serious and I could still conceive. So I kept trying but nothing worked. I didn't tell my husband about the fibroid.

Last December, he traveled to our state to see his people. Couple of months after he came back, he told me there's another woman pregnant with him and he wanted to marry her. To say I was devastated is an understatement. We are Muslims and he's entitled to more than one wife, but I just couldn't take it.

Though he treats me well, I feel there's nothing left for me in the marriage. I am just waiting to sell off the few goods I have in the shop, so I can have some money to sustain myself while I go back to my family."

AYSA

"I never knew we would get to this level as a country. I used to think it's something we would just overcome within a short while but that's not the case.

I'm a salary earner. I started a provision shop for my wife immediately we got married so that she too can have a reliable means of income to support the family once in a while

When this particular government came into power with all their campaign promises,we all thought that things would work out for the masses but things didn't turn out that way;rather, we went from bad to worse.

For the past six years, nothing has improved in this country. My salary has remained the same. It's even worse with inflation. When you try to demand for a salary increase,the response you get will leave you heartbroken. I am actually looking at joining my wife in the provision business but with the state of the country,one needs more than three streams of income to meet up with bills.

This election period has really taught me some lessons about these politicians and their cohorts. They don't care about the welfare of people neither do they have the interest of the country at heart. Universities have been on strike for a long time and these people are shamelessly coughing out huge sums of money to purchase forms.

The one that hurts me the most is that about 89% of the students that are directly affected don't even have a PVC and they have no interest in getting one.

I believe this is the reason why the country is where it is today. It would only take the mercy of God to get us out of this mess we're in this country. If not, generations yet unborn won't have a place to call a country. We are in a deep mess, but we all act as if everything is normal.``

REBECCA

"This business belongs to my husband. When we were dating, I would stop by to visit him and in the process watch how he'd bargain and sell to customers. A couple of times, I went with him to the abattoir.

After we got married, I continued to visit him, especially when I was pregnant and was asked not to do anything. To ease off the boredom, I'd come and sit with him.

Last December, my husband was involved in an accident that almost took his life. He was bedridden for months and only started walking again.

Because I wasn't doing anything, we had to rely on our savings and support from family and friends. But there's a limit both sources can take us and we would run out of money. I suggested to my husband to let me restart his business. He laughed it off, but when he saw I was serious, he refused. He said it wasn't a business for women. I told him he could make all the arrangements over the phone and I'd only go to pick up. Besides, his customers have been asking when he'd return and he may end up losing them all. He accepted grudgingly and I started.

It's not been easy, but we're getting money and when he's fully back on his feet, he won't have to struggle to get his business back on track.

DANIELLA

"We had met at the admissions office where we had both gone for clearance and we connected immediately. We did everything together and at the end, we got assigned to the same room.

Over time, we got to know about each other. I knew her parents were divorced. She told me how her dad constantly abused them until he eventually abandoned them. Her mom was the one struggling to foot her bills. I, on the other hand, was comfortable and I never had to struggle for anything even though I didn't come from a wealthy family. My home was also a happy one. Because I knew she lacked parental love, I tried to pull her into my family. I'd get my parents to speak with her. I was also interested in meeting her family, and would ask to speak with her mum when she called, but she never allowed it.

By our third year, I had gotten an accomodation and left the hostel. She went with me. I was doing a lot of freelancing so I was making money for myself. I supported her financially. One time she couldn't pay her fees, I helped her with the money. She was always secretive and kept to herself. She wouldn't date, she wouldn't make friends. I assumed it was because of her family background and I tried to talk her out of it. Other than this, she was a very nice person and very supportive.

After we graduated, we both remained in the town. I did it because of my business at the time, but she stayed because she just didn't want to go back home.

Later I got a business offer in another city and decided to move. I told her about this, left most of my properties for her and left.

Few months later, she told me she was coming to the city too. I had not gotten an accomodation and was staying with a friend. I told her I couldn't ask them to accommodate her too, but I could ask another lady who was looking for someone to share rent with. I spoke with the lady and she agreed to accommodate her.

After a while, she started complaining about how dirty the lady was, but I kept encouraging her to stay till she could get a better place. All of a sudden, she stopped taking my calls. I'd send messages and she won't reply. Then she blocked me on social media. Twice I asked the lady she's staying with to take the phone to her, the feedback I got was that she didn't want to speak with me. I was surprised at first because I didn't understand where the attitude was coming from.

When I kept trying to reach her to no avail, the surprise turned to hurt. I wanted to know what I did or must have said wrong, so I could make amends. Weeks turned to months and then years went by.

I traveled out for my Masters and returned. Still, no news from her. But every day I prayed that she'd be fine and doing well wherever she was.

I ran into friends from university and they told me they saw her and had asked about me and she said I was okay. I didn't tell them we had not spoken for over two years.

I went back home that day and cried. I didn't know the heart could hurt from friendship breakup. I really liked her and miss her. Though I still wish to know what I did wrong, so I can have closure, I have learnt to move on and I wish her well. "

HAJIYA

"I got married to the love of my life 28 years ago and we have been living in peace. Sometimes there are some challenges but as couples we make things work out the way we want it to.

My husband and I are of different ethnic and religious backgrounds. We became friends right from our secondary school days. I liked him because he was intelligent and was a friend to everyone.

I could still remember how I invited him to my house to meet my parents and siblings after our WAEC exams. The day he came, everyone in my family liked him.

I gained admission into the university before him. A year later, he also got admission in the same university. We re-united again and that was how our friendship blossomed into a relationship.

After we graduated, we still kept in touch. There were no mobile phones then. It was via letter writing.

When he asked for my hand in marriage,I was scared that it wasn't going to work out,but after so many consultations and persistence, it finally came to pass. My husband promised that he would allow me practice my faith, that it won't be a barrier and he has kept to his words till date.

God blessed our union with four children and two of them are graduates.When I was about to get married to him, some friends and family members almost made me not to, but today I'm glad I did.

If I'm asked to do it again,I will do it a million times over. I found love and peace in the strangest place. Nothing gives me joy more than my family

WILSON

"Gone are the days when a man could easily assault his wife and get away with it. Few days ago, my neighbor came back very late and I guess he was drunk. The wife refused to open the door for him. He knocked for several minutes before one of our neighbors intervened and the wife opened the door.

Immediately, this man gave his wife two resounding slaps right before the neighbor that intervened. The next thing we heard was the man calling for help. Before we could rush downstairs to know what's happening, our neighbor has given him the beating of his life.

When everyone came out, one of the neighbors insisted that the man wouldn't sleep in his house because he would end up beating the wife and no one would come to her aid. The man had to sleep outside till the next morning.

The following day, the man called the whole neighbor in the compound and apologized. I was so happy because someone was able to stand up for the woman and at the same time, taught the abuser a lesson he would never forget in a hurry.

I have noticed that these few days, the man no longer keep late nights and his attitude towards his wife and kids has really improved.

One thing I think that can completely reduce domestic violence is confronting the abusers with the same energy and approach they use on their victims. It will help curb domestic violence.

SEKINAT

"After I broke up with my child's father, I thought that was the end for me relationship wise. It was the fear that no man would want me after a child that made me move in with him in the first place. He would abuse me both physically and verbally. Most times, he wouldn't give me any money for food. What saved me and my daughter from starving was my business. I continued to stay hoping he would come see my parents like he promised, but he never did.

When my daughter was 3 years old, I got tired of his attitude towards us and decided to leave. I had given up on relationships. I concentrated on my business and my daughter and moved on.

Four years later, when this man started asking me out, I thought he wasn't serious. He had come visiting his brother who was my neighbor. He would come to my house to help with chores. He would prepare my child for school and would even offer to take her while I went to my shop.

After he left, he kept in touch. He started coming more often and eventually moved in with his brother. When my niece came to live with me, he never complained. Since his job was flexible, he had more time on his hands. I practically left the two kids to him. He would even prepare dinner before I get back.

For the first time, I was being pampered with someone going out of his way to please me. He didn't just support work around the house, he supported it with money too. We've been dating for a year now and he has already gone to see my family and take the traditional marriage list.

Right now, we are house hunting and also preparing for the wedding ceremony which will be done by the end of the year."

FERDINAND

"We used to live in the same compound in Lagos back in 2002 before I traveled abroad. I visited Nigeria back in 2018 and the spirit told me to go and look for her widowed mother. I went and found out life has been rough for them. I invited her to where I lodged, gave her some money, and also promised to be taking care of her when I traveled back.

I have kept to this promise by sending her money since 2018. I also promised to send her to a skill acquisition center when I return this year. She is the only daughter with two brothers. I started talking to her about marriage since I have known her and her family for a long time. I was planning to marry her and rent a three bedroom apartment for her and her mother so they can move out of the one bedroom they currently live in.

I spoke to a friend about my intentions to marry her and he told me not to try it, that she's not a good girl. I have never listened to my friend because I like to see before believing and not act based on hearsay. Her birthday was on the 15th of May and I sent her money to get a cake. Before her birthday, she got sick and was taking native medications before I sent her money to get a proper treatment.

On her birthday, I called to talk to her and her friend picked the call and told me that she went to buy something. I told her friend to inform her I called but to my surprise, the call and others after that were not returned. I called her mom later that night and was informed she had gone to bed.

Good men are everywhere, but when God is giving them to women, they don't always accept them. She's from another state and though people always say we do not marry from her state, I thought it would work out, so I can refute those claims. I'm beginning to think my friend could be right after all.

For now, I have channeled my mind back to my state. I will continue to help her widowed mom in any way I can but for marriage with her, I do not think it will happen."

NANCY

"My mistake was in not showing too much interest in finding out what he actually did for a living . When we started dating, he told me he was working for a construction company before he was laid off and currently into different businesses. I saw him as a young man working very hard and doing well for himself. We went out almost every evening and he would spend so much.

The day I found out what he did for a living, we had gone out as usual. On our way, we sighted NDLEA officers at a Police checkpoint. He quickly gave me a small envelope and instructed me to put it under my blouse. It happened so fast that I started wondering where he brought it out from. After we passed the officers, he asked if I knew what he had given me and then told me it was cocaine. He told me how he was introduced to the business when he was running taxi services at the airport. After that day, I started thinking of a way to cut off from him without raising dust.

During that period, I followed him to his business dealings. He said he trusted me and knew I would never betray him. He taught me the names of all the drugs. Prior to that time, I didn't know there were varieties. I saw very young girls in private schools pay hundreds of thousands on drugs. I saw politicians and respected people in the society. The one that shocked me the most was a lead singer in one of these popular churches. He said he didn't believe it when she told him she sang in the choir till she invited him.

To satisfy my own curiosity, I followed him to the church one evening after he had sold it to her. I opened my mouth wide, staring at her as she sang and spoke in tongues. Funnily enough, he himself didn't take any.

Gradually, I started pulling away. Whenever he called, I'd look for an excuse. If he came by my house, I'd tell him I wasn't around. He tried to talk me out of breaking up with him but my constant avoidance and not responding to him finally made him let me go.

While I was still with him, I tried to make him stop but that was his source of livelihood and it paid well. Nothing I said got to him. The temptation to just stay with him and be careful was there, but I knew the risk involved and wouldn't want to be made a scapegoat for something I have no hand in. "

ONYEKA

"I'm more concerned about my well-being and my business. I don't have a social life and I barely keep friends.

After my secondary school, I was asked to go and serve my master. I served him for six years and after that, he settled and blessed me.

For those six years, my life revolved around one circle which is from the house to the shop and from the shop back to the house. The only time I moved out of my environment was when traveling to Onitsha or Lagos to purchase some goods.

This is my fourth year as my own boss and I'm thinking of getting married, but it has been quite a difficult task for me. I have not been able to get along in my relationship. My fiancée always complains that I don't have time for her,that it's not about providing all her needs, but I need to be spending some quality time with her. I have really tried to do that, but it's not my thing. I hardly go out and each time she schedules for us to go out, it doesn't favor me because from Monday to Saturday, I'm in my shop and Sunday is the only day I have time for myself. I usually rest and plan for the week ahead on Sundays.

Honestly it's affecting me because I see some of my business partners the way they socialize and still run their business smoothly. I guess my behavior stems from the way my master trained us. I'm doing very well in business, but I think I need to improve my social life. I need to learn how to balance both and also not make my wife feel neglected by the time I get married."

IFEANYI

"Back then, even people without degrees were well paid. I didn't go to school. I had gotten in as a casual staff before I worked my way fully into the company. I was doing well at least by my family standard and people around me. Coming from a poor background, it was a great feeling to be able to afford some things I could not while I was still in the village.

I had already stayed with the company for years when the money doubling scheme came into town. They promised to increase our money in months through paying interests. Their offer was so mouth watering that people were throwing in their life savings. I was skeptical of it until two of my colleagues took voluntary retirement and put in the money in the scheme.

After the first month, they came back with testimonies of the money they received as interest. I decided to join them. I told my brother about it and he discouraged me. There was nothing he didn't say. He even pleaded with me, but I felt he was jealous and became more adamant. I applied for voluntary retirement, took the money, and put all of it into the scheme.

Few months later, the people disappeared. Nobody knew anything about them or how to trace them. We didn't have phones then so other than going to their office, there was no other way to reach them.

I almost died during that period. I didn't know where to start. The company wouldn't take me back.

Many years have passed and I still haven't been able to get back to that level. It has been from one struggle to another. My brother never really forgave me for that and it affected our relationship. That mistake is the biggest regret in my life and I find it hard to forgive myself."

KATE

"I'm a mother of two. My husband lost his job during the covid-19 period in 2020. He was working as a personal driver to one expatriate who is an engineer with a telecom company.

Everything was moving fine for us until that covid-19 period. My husband's boss tested positive for the virus. After his isolation and treatment, he decided to return back to his home country and that was how my husband lost his job.

When he was still working, he registered me in a catering school to learn how to make cakes,snacks,different kinds of fruit juice, and smoothies. Then he was the one taking care of all the bills from house rent,the kids' school fees and other utility bills.

Since he lost his job, things haven't really been easy for us. I have graduated from my catering school. I have been getting some cake jobs but because I don't have all the equipment, especially the oven, I give out some jobs to my former course mates. They usually give me a percentage from the amount I charged.

My husband has also been searching for jobs, but he is yet to get one. What he does most times is go out to do some site work and get his day pay. That's how we have been taking care of our kids and bills.

Each day that passes by, I pray to God to help my husband secure another job. From the little money I make, I'm saving some to purchase baking equipment. I need to start production instead of giving out the jobs I get. I produce 30 egg rolls daily and supply them to outlets. That's how I make my own money.

God has been faithful to me. All the people I supply to do sell out everything everyday. I know that if my husband gets another job, he won't hesitate to buy me all the equipment I need. That's why I always pray to God to help him get a job.

NKAY

"We had been friends since childhood and shared secrets. I knew who she was dating at every point and vice versa. As we grew older, she started dating this very handsome guy. He was doing well though not in a way you would classify as rich.

In the course of that relationship, another man, very wealthy, started asking her out. As always, she told me about it, seeking my advice. Knowing her poor background and how she had been struggling to come out of it, I advised her to go with the wealthy man. Her problem was that the man was not good looking at all, but I encouraged her to ignore his looks and focus on the wealth. She finally accepted his proposal and they started making marriage plans.

A week into her marriage, she decided to pay a visit to the handsome boyfriend to inform him of her marriage and break up with him. She told me about this also. Some hours after she left, she sent a message telling me the boyfriend had locked her in.

Shortly after that, I couldn't reach her again. By the end of that day, she was not back home. Her fiancé and family members have all tried reaching her, but the number was switched off. They called me to ask about her, but I denied knowing her whereabouts. I should have told them then, but I wasn't thinking straight. The only thing on my mind was how to keep the fiancé from knowing where she had gone. I didn't even think that she could be in danger.

24 hours later, she was still not back. They decided to report at the Police Station. I was invited for questioning, but I kept denying any knowledge of her whereabouts. I was locked up, threatened, hit a few times. There was no word of abuse, the police didn't rain on me. Everyone was of the opinion that I had planned for my friend's kidnap out of jealousy. Even my boyfriend was called to talk to me, but I still refused.

I stayed in the cell for 3 days. By this time, I felt it was already too late for me to open up and was just praying that my friend would come back safely.

On the 3rd day, she came out and when she was told what had transpired, she came straight to the police station to see me. Immediately I was brought out, I broke down in tears. I asked her what happened and she told me the guy had locked her up, seized her phone and for those three days, he was having sex with her non-stop in very violent ways. He wanted to hurt her badly for breaking up with him. I asked her what she told her people and she said she lied to them that she had gone for a church program and they were asked to switch off phones. Somehow they believed her. She apologized to me and made me a promise not to ever reveal what happened.Everyone soon forgot what happened and we moved on.

Her wedding was held and to my surprise, the ex-boyfriend attended. He came to me boasting about what he did to her and shaming her for marrying an ugly man. Listening to him, I was happy my friend left him though she didn't do it in the right way.

After the wedding, I told her that if I ever hear that she kept up any kind of communication with the guy, I would tell everyone what actually happened that day.

It's been years now, I am married too and nobody has heard the truth. Sometimes I feel guilty but other times, I feel like I did right by my friend."

ENDURANCE

"When I traveled out for my Masters abroad, the plan was to stay there after school and not come back to Nigeria except for visits. I was on scholarship, but the scholarship could only take care of my one year fees and I had chosen a two year program. It meant I had to work out the extra fees myself.

Luckily for me ,I had good skills that got me good paying jobs and I was able to save and pay my fees and other bills.I also saved the money required to be in my account for my application for Permanent Residence.

Everything was working out fine.

Then my siblings told me about MBA and encouraged me to invest. I took all of the 10,000 dollars I had saved and put into it. The idea was to keep the money safe till the time I'd need it while also generating more money from it.

Unfortunately, my MBA went down and so did my money. I was left with nothing. Whatever I worked out went into my accomodation and feeding. I applied for the Permanent Residence but was denied on the grounds that I didn't have the required funds in my account. I was asked to go back home and apply again when I have the money. I tried to stay back for a while, but it wasn't easy so I finally decided to come back so I can restrategize and plan my life again.

The loss affected me badly, but I have moved on. If I continue to dwell on it, I won't have the clear mindset to think. I took my lessons, came back home and started from where I left. I have a good plan and I know that with God's help, it will materialize and I'll go back to pursuing my dreams. "

LARRY

"Sometimes I don't blame people that say they'd rather do a man favor than a woman. My story might serve as a lesson to someone out there.

I met my wife when she had nothing to do. I established a small business (laundry and boutique)with the money I had at hand then because I'm a handyman—I do all kinds of interior and exterior decor jobs and my work is based on contract— we both manage to grow the business.

From the proceeds we got from the business, we feed,pay rent and other utility bills. I felt that the proceeds from the business was not really enough to provide our needs, so I had to look for a job that would at least give me a steady monthly income. I also reached out to people I know to help me with job openings that my wife could apply to.

Finally, a family member informed me of a job opportunity in her company, they were planning to establish a branch here in Abuja. She said the company would prefer a lady but she would talk to the director to employ me. Immediately, I told her not to worry about talking to the director, that my wife should take the job. Two days after our discussion, she asked me to tell my wife to call for more details about the job.

Two weeks later, my wife resumed work as the regional manager. I was so happy because I believed God had answered our prayers. I continued with my own job and business.

After two years, my wife suggested buying land in one of the developing areas for us to build our own house and stop paying rent. I told her that my income for now wouldn't really carry a building project. In response, she said she was going to support the project. We got land and built the house.

After we moved into our house, my wife's attitude changed towards me. Out of nowhere, she started accusing me of cheating. If I should talk to a lady over the phone, she would conclude that I was cheating on her.

I had to cut off all my female friends because of my wife so that peace would reign. The recent one she has come up with is that at any little misunderstanding, she would insult me and do everything to provoke me to lay my hands on her so that she can accuse me of domestic violence, but what I do is to just walk away from her and avoid any physical contact with her throughout that day.

I have asked her on several occasions what the problem is, but she has no reasonable idea to give. There was a time I got a contract job and I needed 170,000 naira to complete it and get my payment. I approached my wife to assist me,but she told me she didn't have money. I had to take a loan from someone and completed that job.

Sometimes the kids' beverages would run out and I wouldn't have money at hand, but when I ask her to buy, she would say she doesn't have. I sometimes go the extra mile to provide. Most times I go out to construction sites to carry bricks and stones. Sometimes I collect my friend's car and do cab rides. That's how I keep my family running till month end before I receive my salary where I work part time.

The only reason I'm just being calm is because I want my two kids to be up to 8 and 6 years respectively and I will just call it quits. Sometimes she links up with her ex. They are always discussing when to meet and make out. I already have evidence and I'm just waiting for them to conclude their plans. She is guilty of everything she's accusing me of.

I don't regret ever getting her the job that has given her the money that's making her behave this way. Some women are just ëvil. They will pretend to be with you to get what they want and once they feel they are okay,the next thing is to start blackmailing you and looking for a way to cut you off. Some men are like that too but that shouldn't make you lose hope in humans because there are still a few good and honest people out there.

The only reason that could ever make me quit my marriage is cheating and I will never engage in such. And if my partner cheats, that's the end of the relationship because this is what I made as a covenant to myself before getting married."

HOPE

I am 26 years old. The one man who I trusted dealt me a terrible blow.I've been seeing this guy since 2016. We went through a lot together. When I met him, he wasn't working. I had to make a lot of sacrifices for him. I'm the kind of girl who does not date for dating sake so I stayed with him even though he had nothing. I supported him in cash and in kind. I prayed for him and encouraged him. I cried when he cried. I practically built my world around him.

Though ASUU is on strike, my family asked me not to return home, but I did because of him. Only for me to get here to receive a heartbreak. I'm so in pain because I asked him over and over again if he had something to do with that particular girl. He'd look me in the eye and lie to me. I only discovered the truth on Easter Sunday.

He had posted her on his status with the caption 'Easter gift' with plenty of emojis. I asked him what that was about since he's been denying having anything to do with her. His response broke my heart. He said, "I do not have anything to tell you, just do whatever comes to your mind."

I asked for us to see and talk. He came and told me to move on. How do I do that? After giving him 6 years of my life, my money, my time and body. He left me for a girl he met barely 4 months ago and all he could say was I should please forgive him. How do I forgive him when I've not even forgiven myself for being a joke?

I don't know how to forgive him.He has broken me.He has broken my heart in places I never knew existed.I'm hurting.

I don't know how to start all over.I thought he had my back but now I have realized I was the clown in the circus, the joke was on me.How could he do this to me when all I did was love him?I need prayers to help me forgive him and the grace to forge ahead."

MARK

"Life has really dealt me a heavy blow. I have never been in this kind of situation before in my life. I'm praying and wishing for God to just bring me out of it stronger and better.

Four months ago, I fell down from a scaffold while I was working to earn my daily bread. I have been working day in day out to raise money for my wife's childbirth because she was booked for a cesarean section. I never wanted to be caught unaware, so I had to plan ahead. But you know we are humans; as we are busy making our own plan, God is busy making his own plan. The money I was saving for my wife's childbirth was what I used to treat myself.

Two weeks ago, my wife gave birth through CS and she is still in the hospital. My happiness is that she and the baby are doing fine. Out of the 150,000 naira the hospital charged me, I have been able to pay 60,000 naira out of it. I have no other choice than to resume work. Even though I have not fully recovered, I have to go out and look for the money I will use to discharge my wife and child. These are the challenges and phases a man must pass through in life.

I am not losing hope because I know I will surely overcome this phase. It's only time it will take, but I will surely overcome it."

AUGUSTINE

"Last year, I shared a story here of how I single-handedly sponsored my NCE programme through farming, and how I intend furthering my education.

I got a job last December in a factory, but it was not easy at all, especially as I'm allergic to dust and cold. But because I needed the money, I had to take the job. We were to be paid 45,000 naira, but the boss in my department decided to be paying us 20,000 naira. My transport took up a large part of the pay. In three months, I was only able to save 30,000. We worked long hours and my boss was always shouting at us,so I decided to quit.

Immediately I quit the job, I traveled to the village back to farming. Initially, I thought of hiring laborers to clear the land for me, but I also needed money to make ridges, so I decided to clear the land myself. I spent 7 days clearing, then hired laborers to make the ridges. After that, I planted cassava, maize and melon.

The stress soon affected my health and I had to take care of it with the little money left. The work I did was already affecting me. I used some money to take care of my health. I also applied for my degree programme, which by God's grace, I will be starting next year.

I love farming, I don't like seeing people hungry since God created more than enough. If only I have the right farm machines, it will really help but since I do not have one, I'll keep doing it this manual way.

When it is time for harvest, I will sell some to pay for my school fees, and I will also give out to those who are hungry. Since I'm done with the planting for now, I need to work again, to also save more money for my programme next year.

My plan is to look for a teaching job but any other job I find that won't affect my health will also be fine. "

JACINTA

"I have been in this security job for four years now and I'm happy with it. When I first came to Abuja, I was into buying and selling clothes. I used to carry my goods from one office to another. The business was thriving but due to debts incurred from customers not paying as at when due, my capital for the business was lost. I started applying for jobs but couldn't get one.

Finally when this security job came up, I was not really interested in taking it, but my friend made me accept the job. At first I was ashamed to take the job. I was worried about what people would say, but my friend told me one thing that made me grab the job offer with both hands. That day she called me and said that I should remember that nobody would pay my bills and that I shouldn't live my life to impress people rather I should live to impress myself.

On the interview day, I was surprised to see more ladies both single and married that applied for the job whereas I was given a slot and I was still doing as if they were forcing me to take the job. After the interview, I just promised myself that I will never live my life to impress anyone and I will stop worrying myself over what people will say because the same people would laugh at you when you can't pay your bills.

My advice to everyone out there is to make sure that you do what is right as long as you can pay your bills off it. Take care of yourself and not engage in any kind of crime.

BEULAH

"It had been my turn the previous day. I had gone to sweep as early as 5am and by 6:30am, I was done. The next day was my friend's turn. We attended the same church and also lived on the same street. We had started the job together. Someone who worked in the government got us employed as a way of empowering the widows in the church.

That morning, I was still sleeping when I started hearing screams outside. At first, I thought it was robbers or maybe people fighting. When I paid more attention, I realized it was actually the wailing I was hearing. I was already getting dressed to go find out what was happening when my teenage son rushed into the bedroom. He told me not to come out. I insisted on knowing what the matter was but he ran back out locking me inside.

I was very angry but there was nothing I could do. I didn't have a phone then so there was no way to call anybody to know what was happening. About thirty minutes later my son came back with two neighbors. They sat me down, warned me not to shout or cry and then broke the news to me.My friend had gone out to work as usual. While sweeping, a car came charging towards her and before she could even realize what was happening, it had knocked her over. She died on the spot. The hit and run driver was never caught. The rest of us didn't wait to be told to stop the job.

It took me years to get over the incident. I couldn't help thinking it could have been me. The job was only revived when a new government came in. Most of us that had left went back but only after they agreed we could start work when it's already daylight. I have moved away from that area and here the traffic isn't much and we are also very careful. It is not the best job but it puts food on the table without having to beg."

SAM

"I wrote my WAEC exams ten years ago. Now that I finally decided to go back to school to further my education,they went on strike. I thought it wouldn't last more than a month but unfortunately the government has been less concerned and acting as if everything is okay.

What hurts me the most is that these politicians still have the guts to go about campaigning while ignoring the fact that the future of the youths has been put on hold by their nonchalant attitude. When these youths decide to go into crime due to frustration,the society will blame them without looking at the root cause of the whole situation.

Since the government doesn't want to do anything about the strike, I have decided to go out there and get something done to stay away from crime and trouble. Each day I go out,I come back home with at least 3,000 naira. I have been saving some parts of my daily earnings so that whenever they decide to call off the strike, I would have raised enough money for my school fees and basic needs. If they decide that they won't do anything about it, I will just forget about going to school and look for something meaningful to do with my life.

Honestly, this country is frustrating the citizens, especially the youths. That's why 9 out of every 10 young people you approach will tell you they want to leave the country and go to a place where human life is more valued. The government should act fast and amend most parts of the constitution to make a provision for the youths of this nation who are potential leaders of tomorrow.

FAITH

"When I look at how the standard of education has deteriorated, I worry for my children.

While growing up, I went to a Federal Government school. They were not perfect, but they were good. Teachers were strict and you dare not misbehave . The teaching was good too because our teachers back then were well trained. But now, the standard of education is nothing to write home about. Private schools are springing up everywhere and most of them are just out to extort money from parents.

My child is 6 years old and in primary one. When we got the list for his school materials for that session, I saw a laptop. At first I thought they meant a tablet for kids, so I had to call for clarification. To my surprise, they maintained that it's a laptop they need. I asked them what a six year old would be doing with a laptop and they started mentioning so many things. Left to me alone, I wouldn't have bought it, but my husband said we should give it a try.

Couple of months after we bought the laptop, the teacher called that it wasn't working anymore. My first thought was that they probably didn't handle it properly because it was a brand new laptop. My husband took it to his colleague who was into tech, but the guy couldn't figure out what was wrong. It was when my husband took it to a laptop repairs that it was discovered the hard drive had been removed. We went back to the school to confront them. Of course they denied it. I was just so angry I had to change my son's school. I never trusted their request in the first place and for that to happen, I couldn't continue to leave my child in their care.

One just has to be very careful about the kind of school and people we expose our kids to. In as much as we have a part to play in their training, these people also play a major role and someone who lacks integrity is already a bad sign."

CHIDERA

"Relocating to Abuja was one of the biggest decisions I have ever made in my life. Although it wasn't easy,I had lots of setbacks and challenges, I never gave up on that dream.

After my Education down south,I began to think of how to better my life and establish my future as I have always wanted. I had saved up some amount of money. I told my mother and my siblings that I would like to change the environment. I have spent almost 25 years of my life down south. I needed to move and start up my life in a new environment. They all said it was a good idea and asked how I'd cope with the arrangement. My sister said house rent in Abuja was expensive and cost of living was also high. I just told them not to bother,that I'd definitely make a way for myself to survive.

The first ten months here weren't easy for me. I kept on pushing till my hard work paid off. I started off with a salary of 20,000 naira. I was working in a bakery and they gave me accommodation. I worked there for four years and was able to save up enough money from my salary. Because I wasn't paying house rent, the only expenses I was making was just feeding and some money I was sending back home

When I wanted to quit the job, I informed my boss. She said it was not going to be a problem since I worked for her for four years and there was no issue. She said I could still be staying in the company apartment till I was ready to pack out. I was filled with joy.

The money I budgeted for house rent,I used it to purchase extra goods and added to my shop. Till now, I am still staying in the apartment my boss gave me. She said it's her own way of paying me back for all the services I rendered to the company for four years.

I sell foodstuff in the market. I have also brought my younger brother down to Abuja and I introduced him to my boss. Currently, he is working in the bakery and I have also been putting him through. I encourage him to do better than me. To be successful in life, I think the basic principle is to be focused and know what you want."

SHALOM

"I will be 31 years old by November. I have been fending for myself for a long time because I lost my father at a young age. I had to work extra hard to see myself through school.

Ever since my graduation in 2019, I haven't gotten any job though I have applied to several organizations both online and in person. Luckily for me, I got shortlisted into the Npower program and that is what has been sustaining me. I also enrolled in a tailoring class to get the skill but frequent chest pain won't let me concentrate.

In November last year, I had a terrible pain which I prayed about. After a week, I went to the hospital for a checkup. I was told I had an ulcer, but it wasn't serious. I went back two weeks later and got the same result meanwhile the pain just got worse.

While I was still thinking of my health, the friend I've been staying with asked me to leave. I pleaded for a month to sort myself out. The issue affected me both physically and mentally. I couldn't even attend my classes anymore as I spent my days searching for accomodation.

I have been thinking about why I have to go through all these. No job, no house, no marriage. I lost happiness long ago. I feel I need special prayers to succeed and for my debtors to pay, so I can go for a check-up in another hospital before it gets out of hand."

EZINNE

"Being a caregiver is by far one of the most challenging positions. It requires a lot of learning, trial and error as well as lifestyle shifts. And with that responsibility comes the feelings of exhaustion, sadness, and more.

I am a student of Imo State University, Owerri and the first child of my family. I have been living with my sick brother (diagnosed with brain tumor) in the hostel since last year. Due to my family background, we can't afford money for his surgery and the services of a nurse to be taking care of him, so he's living in the hostel with me since there's no one to take care of him at home.

My mom is late and where my dad trades is far from home. When I agreed, I didn't know it would be this tough. My life instantly changed. People see me as this strong girl, but they don't know I am only faking it. It's only my room and pillow that know the amount of pain I hide from the world.Most times I miss lectures and tests. I am hardly in any social gathering because whenever I'm out, my mind is always unsettled as I don't know what is going on with him.

Some nights we don't sleep well because of seizures that keep recurring.

There are times when I get very sad because I see my friends and peers achieving their dreams, starting up businesses, doing one thing or the other to secure their future whereas I cannot do any of those because of my brother. I tried working on different occasions, but my bosses didn't understand when I told them about my brother's health issues and how it was making me late for work so they sacked me on different occasions.

There were times I just want to give in to peer pressure and go into prostitution— times when my dad won't send us money for weeks and my brother would need to take drugs but no food available, times when I'd need to buy textbooks and pay for practicals, times when there was no one to talk to. The only boyfriend I had broke up with me when he saw my brother, but God keeps helping us out.

One of my greatest fears is life after school because I don't know what the future holds. I really wish to learn a skill. Now we are on strike. I really want to use this opportunity to learn catering as I have the passion but I don't have the financial support and resources for that.

That I have come this far is only by the grace of God and I really pray life gets better for my family and I because we have been through a lot. Say a word of prayer for us. "

JAMES

With the recent happenings and news about domestic violence in marriages,I have decided to share my own story as a man who has endured every form of abuse from his wife since the first month of our marriage till date.

Our marriage is just three years old. My wife knows very well that I'm a handy man and it's what I get from my work I use in taking care of the family. I was the one who helped her get her job. I sold my car to finance our wedding. My wife only bought the asoebi clothes she gave her sisters. That was her only contribution.

Since we have been in this marriage, she insults me at any given opportunity. She would use so many demeaning words on me. I don't usually react,all I do is walk away.

What she does with her income is none of my business,but anytime I send money to my family members, she would just pick a fight,abuse me and say all sorts of heartbreaking things to me. This is someone that most times when I get a contract,she would never support me. She would rather watch me source for funds from family members and close friends, but when I decide to appreciate those people that stick out their neck for me, she starts complaining.

One thing I learnt earlier is to never ask her for help or support of any kind because whenever she buys even if it's water at home, she would ask me for a refund. The best way I decided to handle her is to just ignore her, focus more on my life, and that of my children.

Ever since we got married, her actions have made me stop communicating with my friends, both male and female. If I should talk to any lady,she would ask me what I'm discussing with the person. Most times we do come across some of my classmates and childhood friends and she would feel so insecure.

Sometime ago, she made me lose out on a contract I had gotten and a part payment has been made already. I was in the bathroom, my phone rang, and she picked up the call. When she heard a lady's voice, she started insulting her over the phone.

I came out and I asked who she was on the phone with. I checked my phone and saw who called,I told her it's the lady that had the project I was to commence work on that day. While we were still discussing, a text message came in from the same lady asking me to refund the part payment for the job. That was when she realized the consequences of her action. Right there in her presence, I transferred back the money. That was how I lost that contract. The person that referred me to the client called and was asking me what happened,I just told him it was my wife.

People have asked me to divorce her. I don't want to separate my children from their mother, they are still too tender. I have promised myself that I would never raise my hands or voice at her because as a child, I never for once saw my dad raise his voice at my mum nor even hit her and I don't think anyone can change me or make me do otherwise.

So many men pass through a lot in the hands of their wife,but when they speak out people won't believe them. This is the reason why some have decided to be silent. The best thing to do as a man is to ignore and focus more on your life and that of your kids. Nothing pains a woman more than total silence when she is expecting you to react."

JANE
The major challenge I have in this job is people thinking I cannot give them what they want. Some people will even go as far as looking for fault where there is none just to prove that I didn't do it well and my boss would have done it better. The worst part is when a customer gets his job, sees a fault and immediately assumes I had done the job. It is not all bad though. There are some customers I have proven my skills to and they have come to trust me and even recommend me to friends.

I learnt this skill because I was bored from staying at home for a long time due to strike. I didn't even take it seriously then but when I did my first job for sale and got compliments, I started putting in more effort. I am still learning and I keep improving. It's been two years since I started and whenever I am going on break, I devote my full time to it. Like now that we are on strike and I'm back home, I come here everyday and I have been making some money. By the time school resumes, I would have saved up money to support myself in addition to what my parents would give me.

ADIMOLA

"He was doing quite well when I met him. He was comfortable enough to afford the cost of sending his two brothers abroad though they are back now. He also built the house we are living in now.

Some years after our marriage, he lost his job and things went south from there. He changed from the loving man I used to know to one that is always angry and abusive. From using words, he started using his hands.

At a point, his father started living with us. His father used to be well off too. From what they told me, he squandered his money on women and didn't build any house or even invest in any business. The mechanic workshop he managed to keep, he is not taking it seriously. He goes whenever he likes and when he has money, he does not support us in any way but goes after women.

I have gone hungry several times just so my children and father-in-law could eat. Yet, neither my husband nor his father appreciates my effort. The proceeds of my business got emptied in taking care of the house. My father-in-law has been with us now for over 7 years and the burden on me is just too much. His other sons don't even want to hear any discussion about accommodating him, nor do they show any interest in helping my husband in spite of what he has done for them.

I used to complain about my father-in-law's presence and attitude. I have also suggested he gets a place since he is still strong enough to be going after women. I had to stop and swallow everything when my husband started using it as a reason to hit me. Even when the father is around, he still hits me and the father has never come out of his room any day to intervene.

My husband does NIN registration in a space in my own family compound given to him by my father yet this man insults me and my family at will. Many times, I have thought of leaving but the fear of what will happen to my kids holds me back. He has warned me not to take his children away from his house.

It's been several years of living in hardship and torture and I feel I have had enough. The last incident was what made me decide to leave.I heard about a former neighbor who had relocated to another state and is doing very well. I got his contact and called to ask if he could get a job for my husband. The man had just asked me if we would be willing to relocate and I told him yes, we can come over. When my husband walked in,he heard what I said and started accusing me of planning to go meet a man. Even as I tried to explain, he took off his belt and started flogging me with it. The most embarrassing part was that the call was still on and the man could hear us. I had not eaten that day because the little food I could get, I had given it to my children. I was already very weak even before he started flogging. In all these, his father was inside and never came out. My children tried to intervene, but he pushed them away and warned them not to get up from their seats.

When he was done, I managed to call my father to tell him what was happening. My father was just screaming that he didn't want to see him in his compound where he used to do his business again. I managed to go over to a neighbor's house who took care of me and gave me food. I haven't left the house yet, but I am planning to. I cannot leave my daughters with him either. I plan to take my daughters and leave the boys. Maybe that way, he won't give me too much trouble and I'll be able to take care of myself and the girls."

FRANCES
"I'm eighteen years old and in my second year in university. Before the strike, I used to have this guy that wanted me to be his girlfriend. At first he approached me in the form of a brother because we were from the same state and he was a year ahead of me. When we started getting along,he was so caring and loving. He watched over me as a big brother would watch over his little sister.

One day he invited me over to his place. Actually, we were supposed to meet at a particular time but along the line there was a diary from my own end due to lectures and I got to his place some hours past our agreed time. He already made up his mind that I wasn't going to come.

On getting to his place, I noticed that he had some other guests in his house and they were having a discussion, so I decided to just hang around and to listen to their conversations because their voices were loud. To my greatest surprise, their discussion was not welcoming because all they talked about was how to go pull a hit and how they would be respected after the hit. Lots of conversations that you don't need a soothsayer to tell you that they were cultists. I quietly tiptoed out and left.

Few days later, I was coming out of the lecture hall and we met. He started complaining that I had been avoiding him because I didn't honor his invitation to his place and I didn't even bother to tell him what my reasons were. Immediately I told him that I didn't want to continue with the friendship, he got angry and told me it was not possible, not after watching over me all this while. That I had chosen to turn him down now that he had asked me to be his girlfriend. He said that it won't happen as long as he was still alive and that I won't have any other male friend besides him.

At first I thought he was joking not until he attacked one of my course mates one day on our way back from lectures. That was when I didn't hesitate to inform my parents about the whole thing. My dad immediately went straight to the police, made a complaint, and he was invited over to the station with his parents. He had to write an undertaking, alongside his parents, that he would never step in my way. Also, that if anything should happen to me while I was still in the school, he would be held responsible.

His parents never had any idea that he was a cultist and they were disappointed because the dad lamented that they made sure he never lacked anything. The mum said I should never be bullied into silence, that she admired my courage for informing my parents before it got out of hand.

My parents are our best friends. They made my siblings and I to always confide in them no matter the situation we find ourselves in and that is why we rarely get into trouble.

Parents should learn how to communicate and relate with their children so that they can always be open to communicate their feelings and challenges with them without fear. Till we left school because of the strike, he didn't disturb me for one day. We ladies should also learn to speak out whenever we find ourselves in difficult situations."

UMAR

"Since we began our Ramadan fast, I have constantly prayed to God everyday to change the situation of our country. Each day that passes by, you will definitely hear of a sad incident that occurred somewhere in our country. Honestly I'm tired of the daily bloodshed going on in our country without any remedy from those in charge of the nation's affairs.

If you approached people daily to know their take on Nigeria,you'd find out that the first hundred people you meet have completely lost hope in the country. That is why you see people leaving the country daily. Some take risks to make sure that they are not caught up with the sad happenings in this nation

It's high time the masses came together as one,put aside our religious and tribal differences, and work together to put an end to the reign of all these old politicians who continually rotate power among themselves.

Just yesterday, I bought three oranges for 200 naira and when I asked the man why, he asked if I was expecting him to sell less than what he bought. I can still remember when this present government was about to come to power,agriculture was their key agenda,but it's funny and disheartening at the same time to see that they have invested billions in agriculture and yet foodstuff is the most expensive commodity today in Nigeria.

I just wish my fellow northerners would realize the ruins we are in quickly and act accordingly in the forthcoming elections. I'm tired of the situation in Nigeria, but I won't lose hope because I believe that God is just teaching us some lessons so that we would learn from our mistakes."

JERRY

"I had been waiting for some time at the bus stop with no bus going my way. Just as a bus finally came and I was trying to get in, I felt someone pull me back by the trousers. I turned to see a tout holding my trouser tightly. Before I could ask what the matter was, he hit me with the stick in his hand. People in the bus screamed at him to stop and asked him what I did. He said I was trying to pick pockets. I was too stunned to even know how to react. With the way I was dressed and my looks, how could anyone accuse me of such? He kept hitting me and pulling my trouser. The passengers were still shouting at him to stop and also telling me to get on the bus. He let me go, raining abuses at me and threatening to deal with me next time.

As I got on the bus, some passengers were consoling me while others were angry at me for letting him hit me that way without hitting him back. I was too embarrassed to react. Truth was, violence was not in my nature and it was my first time having a direct encounter with these touts. Besides, I am only visiting here and wouldn't want to get into trouble. That experience shook me and since then, I have avoided bus stops like a plague."

CYPRAIN

"I have always wished to have a smartphone of my own. I'm a POP and wall screeding expert. Most of the people I work with all have a smartphone and they take pictures and make videos of my work. They use it to communicate with customers and get jobs then sub-contract the job to me with little pay.

One day, an engineer I have been talking to about giving me a job called and gave me a three bedroom flat to work on. After I finished the job, the woman was satisfied and from that day she started giving me many jobs to do. From the proceeds I got from the first job she gave me, I purchased an android phone for 30,000 naira. I started taking pictures of my job, so I can also send and show whoever wants my services through WhatsApp.

One of my neighbors advised me to open a Facebook page and telegram, but life has different phases of learning. I am still trying to master how to use the phone effectively to communicate via WhatsApp, so gradually I will also learn how to use those ones my neighbor mentioned to me. I'm filled with joy because I finally got a smartphone of my own and also was able to show people my work whenever I'm asked to bring my catalog."

LOVETH

"When he got employed, I took him in as a younger brother and put him through the ropes. I was working in a sister organization in a similar position as his and both organizations also shared the same building so I knew what the job entailed. At the beginning, he was loyal and respectful. I was also patient to teach him all he needed to know.

A couple of years later, he was no longer as loyal and kept to himself. I felt it was because his pay and working conditions were better than mine. Some years later, I heard they were looking for a replacement for him as he had gotten another job. I approached him to congratulate him and also inform him of my interest to apply. He told me he plans for his wife to replace him, but I could still submit my CV since he won't be the one conducting the interview. I wanted to tell him it wasn't right for his wife to replace him, but I knew he wouldn't take it well so I held my peace.

I submitted my CV and waited for the interview. Weeks later, I had gone to work casually dressed in native and slippers as I used to do on Fridays. I was just entering my office when his colleague saw me and asked why I was not attending the interview. I was surprised because I wasn't invited and had no idea it was going on that day right in the same building. I told the lady and she too was surprised. She went back to her office and after a while came to call me to say that she had spoken to the panel and they accepted for me to join.

Good thing I had a copy of my CV in the office, so I took it and went in to join others. I was very self conscious as I was not properly dressed. Fortunately, the job was something I knew very well so I answered all the questions easily. The panel members were surprised my CV wasn't there in the first place. I didn't need a magician to tell me it was removed.Long story short, I got the job. His wife was not called at all for the interview. I heard his bosses said it was not a family business. He totally stopped talking to me and would even talk rudely to me if we came in contact.

About two years later, he started calling again. From greetings, he started asking for stamps and documents of my organization and would say no each time. He has left the organization, so I do not see why he would still be needing our documents and stamps. Then he started asking for contacts of some top members. I still refused to give him. I finally got to know his job was on contract basis and had ended. I do not know the dubious business he is into and I want to stay out of it.I had helped him once and he paid me back with evil. Even if I want to help him again, it won't be with confidential information from my workplace. "

DOREEN

"My sickness started in 2020. We took it as the usual malaria and started treatment. When it didn't get better, we went for a test but nothing was found.

As the months went by, it became worse and we started going from one hospital to another. Our finances were also dwindling. My husband could not concentrate on his business so nothing was coming in either.

Sometime in February 2021, I was rushed to the hospital. I had given up on life already as I thought that would be my last day. Fortunately, I was stabilized but continued on admission.

One day, I was in a critical condition when my husband's business neighbors called him to let him know his shop was about to be demolished and he should come get his goods out. He told them he couldn't leave me at that point as my life was more important and pleaded with them to help him. Unfortunately, the neighbors didn't give him anything and there's no way of knowing whether or not they removed the goods or let them get destroyed.

I eventually got better and was discharged. By then, we had also gotten a quit notice from our landlady. In all fairness, the woman had tried. We were already owning her one year rent, but she let us go without paying. There was nowhere to go from the hospital. Our church had taken care of most of my hospital bills and didn't have anymore to support us to get a new place. Instead, they offered us a part of the church auditorium to sleep and keep our things. That is where we have been staying since then.

It is very embarrassing because we have to wake up very early to clear the place every day and rearrange it at night. The church may not say it, but I know they may also be tired of the arrangement. The worst thing is that we cannot stay together as husband and wife. We've been married for 8 years without a child. If we are not meeting, how can I even try to get pregnant?

The whole situation has become very humiliating and I'm losing it. My family has since abandoned me. My husband doesn't have many people either.Right now, we have to battle with getting accomodation and also restarting my husband's business.

I am not very strong yet, but I have gone back to my hairdressing business. My husband is also trying and together we have raised some money but not enough for anything yet.

I am hopeful that God who has kept me alive and kept us together throughout all these will still come through for us."

SANDRAH

"We started dating four months ago. When he was asking me out, he didn't even appear serious. His attitude then was just as if he was a playboy,but I decided to give it a try.

After one week of dating, he changed completely; he showed me so much care and love. He always comes to pick me up from home and drop me at my business place. He has been so supportive. Within just four months, he has really impacted me, most especially my business. I was someone that barely had savings but within this short period of meeting him, my life has completely turned around financially. My approach towards business and life entirely has changed.

After my last relationship ended due to genotype incompatibility,I went down on my knees and asked God to take care of the next relationship I would get into. God has answered that prayer by sending him my way. The good news is that he has come to pay my bride price and I'd be relocating to the UK with him. He has already completed every paperwork needed for that. He also made it possible for me to still continue running my business while I'm away.

Most times one door closes for a better door to be opened for us. Instead of wasting time having regrets, just put yourself together, move on, and approach everything with a positive mindset that things would definitely work out for good." -

ANDREW

"When I married my wife, she was healthy with absolutely no health issues. We were living happily until after she had our first child. She lost her mind and had not been in a sane state since then. Because I had no money to take her to the hospital for a proper psychological evaluation since I was just an ordinary cobbler, I resorted to prayer houses. We visited different prayer houses and were told different stories. It was in the process that the only surviving member of her family—her mother—died. She was not sane enough to even understand what was happening, though I still told her about it.

My family members were not pleased with me for still sticking with my wife. I was advised to go and drop her in the market, that's where mad people kept her. To be frank, the thought of dumping her in the market never crossed my mind. That would have been a very cruel act.

So I kept managing with her. At a point, she became a bit better and we went back home and continued our lives as husband and wife. I was basically the one doing everything in the house because I knew she wasn't strong enough.

Many people thought I was crazy for living in the same house with a mad woman. My family neglected me and wouldn't want to have anything to do with me. I was emotionally and financially drained.

Just last year, I heard that the government was reaching out to the mentally disturbed people. When I found out where they were, I took my wife there and she was given an injection which has helped in stabilizing her condition.

We have been on this journey together for over 10 years now. I don't intend to give up. It is for better for worse, till death do us part."

DR.

"It's been nine years since I last visited Nigeria. While I was away, I used to see pictures and videos online of people being harassed and intimidated by security operatives. Most times when I see those videos and pictures, I just conclude within me that it's either they are acting or maybe it's not real, but I almost had a fair share of the harassment and intimidation from the security operatives when I came back.

Two days after I came back, my car was taken to the mechanic for routine maintenance and service. When the mechanic finished the servicing, he called me and pleaded that he won't be able to return the car on time because he had lots of work at hand. I decided to go pick up the car myself from his garage. I took my car and on my way back home, arrived at a checkpoint and the officer ordered me to clear off the road and park, which I did respectfully. One of them carrying a rifle approached me and the first thing he said was:

"Small boy like you dey ride G-wagon. Only God knows how many oyibo you don't steal their money."

I wanted to react immediately, but I just kept my cool so that I'd know his next line of action. Surprisingly, this same officer that's just dressed on black jeans and a pair of dirty black T-shirts asked me to give him my phone. I asked him what he just said so that I would be very sure I heard him correctly. He repeated himself and this time, he tried to raise his hands to slap me. I quickly told him at the top of my voice that if he dared to do that, today would be his last day as a police officer or whichever force he belonged to.

Everyone at the checkpoint, including his fellow officers, were all shocked and quiet. One of them introduced himself as their senior walked up to me and calmed me down. He asked me what the problem was, I narrated everything to him and I also identified myself. They started apologizing and he immediately asked the other officers to collect the rifle from the officer that harassed me and handcuff him. He said the officer was drunk, that I shouldn't be offended. I told him no need for all that because I'd definitely make sure that all of them, including the senior officer, are punished for their reckless behavior and actions towards motorists.

I put a call quickly to their Area command and five minutes later, a team arrived and picked them up and we went straight to the station. If I was just a regular person, I would have been slapped and extorted without committing any crime.

Honestly, our security operatives in this country need a total overhaul and re-orientation on how they should go about their duties, especially those ones that are sent out on routine patrol. They should know that not every young person they see driving a luxury car is into fraud or crime. Most of us work really hard to earn our money and the only way we can appreciate ourselves is to take care of ourselves.

As a doctor, I work virtually round the clock. Sometimes I only have three hours for myself in a day and then when I come back home to rest for my annual leave someone will come to extort me forcefully and label me because they have a gun.

I don't really blame those who are taking the risk to leave this country. If something is not done quickly to fix this mess we're in, we will all wake up one day and will be left with no professionals, especially in the medical field. This country needs to be fixed and that's one of the reasons I like spending my annual leave here in Nigeria. I also use my leave period to organize seminars and carry out free medical outreach in rural areas with some of my colleagues that do visit with me.

MELIE

"Ever since we got married, I've been the one taking care of our bills. I do the shopping for provision and toiletries then give her money for foodstuff.

While we were still living in a rented apartment, I paid the rent. When I eventually got land and built a house, my wife didn't contribute a penny to it. Even as children came, I still took care of all their bills. In all honesty, I did not mind because I believe it's my duty to provide. But with the way the economy is going, I expect that she would pitch in to help.

My wife occupies a top position in a government agency so it's not like she doesn't have money. I have sat her down to ask her what she uses her money for, if maybe she is carrying out a project somewhere I am not aware of. She got offended and didn't give me an answer.

What annoys me now is her penchant for wastage. Everyday, they prepare meals they cannot finish and end up throwing them away. She doesn't even consider the high cost of foodstuff and gas. I have complained several times but she doesn't appear bothered. I don't know if it's because she is not the one bringing out the money.

Very soon, I might have to stop buying anything and watch what she will do. It really hurts me that she behaves this way and I wish she could be understanding and change. "

PROMISE

"I had just finished secondary school and he was already an adult. He was our youth leader. I was new in the church and the general opinion they had of him was that he wasn't a friendly person and should be avoided. I had already decided to mind my business because I was too big for my age and was already getting advances from men.

It happened that I needed a particular textbook and someone told me he could lend it to me. I went to his niece to ask for it and when he heard of it, he insisted I would have to come ask him directly before he would give it out. I did and he agreed to give it to me and even offered to link me to someone who would take me on tutorials in case I was having some challenges in the course. I was pleasantly surprised because that was not the picture people painted. That was how we started talking.

He became overly protective of me and would always want to know everywhere I went to and everything I did. He was also showing favoritism towards me. In all these, I didn't think he had any ulterior motive and just took him as an older brother.

One day, he called me to come meet him at a school. I got there and found the place deserted. It was after school hours so I asked him what he was still doing there. I had not stayed long when he pounced on me trying to kiss and smooch. I struggled with all my strength and then he noticed someone was coming and quickly left me. I felt so bad and left immediately.He later called to apologize.

I was surprised when he called some days later to tell me he had reported himself to the pastor. I was summoned and without asking me what happened, the pastor started berating me. His wife too joined and they called me names saying I was the one who threw myself at him. Since I wasn't there when he made the report, I had no way of knowing what he told them.

The news quickly spread and I became an outcast. I slid into depression, even my friends were mocking me saying I was pretending all along. Some mothers used me as a bad example to their daughters. I couldn't understand it. Even my mother wasn't open for me to talk to. I decided the only way out was to commit suicide. I was ready to do it when I got a text from a secondary school classmate I had exchanged numbers with not too long before then. It was as if she knew what I was going through then. Her words gave me life and that changed my mind.

I am not friends with that classmate but anytime I come across anything concerning her, I am always happy and grateful. Though I have never told her what she did for me. She may not even remember.

I eventually got over that incident and have long left the church, but it made me very reserved. I do not participate in anything. I just go, listen to the preaching and go home. That is the only way I can protect myself from experiencing such accusations again. "

USMAN

"Things have really gotten worse in this country. The prices of goods and commodities have tripled. The government is not even in any way showing concern.

I went to the market today and found that the cost of transporting my goods from the market to my location is now different from what I paid two weeks ago. The price has increased. Commercial drivers no longer buy fuel from the filling station, most of them buy from the roadside sellers because the queue in filling stations is endless.

The prices of goods keep increasing on a daily basis. A carton of biscuits that I used to buy for N800 is now N1, 650. Items that sold for ten naira before are being sold for fifty naira or more and nobody is complaining. Everyone is just acting as if all is well but we all know that all is not well. Now, people only live to survive.

2023 is fast approaching and all these old selfish politicians have already started moving around to declare their intentions. I wish we all could speak with one voice and say no to them. I love this country so much, but the kind of leaders we have has made many lose hope in the country. Anybody you have a conversation with, especially young people, they all want to leave the country and travel out.

I just hope that one day things will get better. I hope we start electing good leaders that would have the interest of this country at heart.

JOHN

"Life has not been easy for me. I'm a WAEC certificate holder. I have written my WAEC exams since 2012. After my exams, I have been doing some casual jobs to take care of my younger ones and myself too. It has not been easy because I'm yet to actualize my dream of getting a good paying job and also raise money and start up a business

Several times, I have been approached by some of my childhood friends saying we should get into crimes like stealing within and outside the neighborhood. I vehemently refused because I wasn't raised that way. My father was a hard working man before he died,so I don't want anything that would tarnish my family's good name. I decided to cut off every friendship I had with any of them.

I have promised myself that I won't allow my situation or the challenges I face in life to ever push me into committing any crime. I will rather work it out than look for a shortcut to success. I know someday I will tell the story of my success as long as I keep my hope alive."

ELLA

"I keep asking myself why things are not falling in place. Maybe I am not praying hard enough. My infant keeps nibbling on my dry breast & the hunger pangs are trying to rip my heart out of my chest. Both won't just let me be.

Everything was planned immediately and we found out that I was with child. He covered all expenses while I was pregnant as I could not work due to some complications. He made sure I fed well and took care of all the bills down to my delivery fee. While at it, he was hastily gathering all papers and documents needed for his exit out of this country. This took a large chunk of his savings.

The plan was for him to leave within January, leaving me with what he had left while he went in search of greener pastures as he repeatedly told me.

He said he didn't want me or our baby to suffer. Baby came before Christmas Eve last year and everything was sorted out. We seemed to have it all under control, earnestly waiting with our optimism at its peak.

However, December passed, so did January and February,but the embassy hasn't called to fix his interview date. We relied on what was remaining of his savings. He had to leave 2 weeks ago to a big city in search of a job. But before he did, he emptied his pockets and gave me (men are not appreciated enough, they are indeed the most selfless being on Earth), promising to send more when he gets a job.

I've been looking for a job too, but no one wants to hire me because my baby is still very tender. And just last week, my health took every dime on me and left me with nothing.

I called him yesterday and he still hasn't found a job. He would be mad at me when he realizes that I shared my story here.

I am hoping that God will come through for me the same way he did in the labor ward when I was slated for emergency CS because I couldn't push,but all of a sudden, I was filled with strength and my baby slipped out.

All I am asking is for him to send an Angel in human form who'll help me with enough to get a Tin or two of my baby's formula and some foodstuff. At Least let me eat and gather strength to continue my search for a job. Hopefully, I'll get one and sort the rest of my bills out.

It's indeed funny how I was in abundance a few weeks ago but right now, I am on the verge of starving to death. Life can be unfair atimes."

BUJO

I was by the road talking with a friend. I didn't see anyone coming. I just felt the sudden pain that almost knocked me off. I think the pain blinded me for a minute. My hand had gone up instinctively to my head where I was hit. The blood was gushing. I was confused and shocked at the same time.

When I got to my senses a little and opened my eyes, what I was hearing was "sorry, sorry." My friend was holding on to the guy who had hit my head with a bottle. They guy said he thought I was someone who had assaulted him. That I was putting on the same cap the person wore and looked like him. I was even in too much pain to make sense of what he was saying. My friend and others who had gathered were already beating him up. Some were saying he should be taken to the police. They had forgotten about me and the fact that I needed medical attention. I had to forcefully pull my friend away from the crowd before he too came to his senses.

In the end, we went to a pharmacy and the guy was made to pay for my treatment. I didn't want to pursue any police case so I let the guy go. But not after my friend had extracted some more cash from him. I have been hearing stories of how people get killed for what they know nothing about, that is what would have happened to me. Maybe nobody would have believed I had nothing to do with the guy. I would have been called names too. I just thank God for the cap. It was what cushioned the effect if not, it would have been worse."

SUNNY

Honestly, this fuel scarcity since January has really dealt me a heavy blow. I have succeeded in not letting the situation change who I am or my personality.

I'm a taxi driver. I'm married with three kids. It's my taxi business I use in taking care of my family and providing all their needs.

Since this fuel scarcity started, it has really affected my business. I spend hours in a queue before I can get fuel. I have refused to hike the cab fare like other taxi drivers. Most of my passengers are normal people like me that either work as salary earners or people that go to work on building sites to look for their daily bread. I have considered that increasing the cab fare would affect them directly and not our leaders who are the cause of the problem this country is facing at the moment.

I believe that it's my good intentions towards people that have been opening doors for me in some areas of my life. One day, I picked a passenger that was going to the federal secretariat. I never knew that he was the husband to the woman that owns the school my kids attend. All through the ride, he enjoyed my joke because I normally engage my passengers with jokes and funny discussions. I feel that it will help some people forget the stress they are going through and be encouraged to carry on.

He was the last passenger to come down from the car when we got to the secretariat. He was shocked that I was still collecting the normal fare from every other passenger. He asked me why and I told him that as long as the pump price has not increased, I don't think it's right for me to increase the fare. He gave me his card and asked me to give him a call. He asked if I could come and pick him and drop him back in an hour and I said I was going to come.

I was surprised when I came to pick him up and he mentioned his destination which happens to be my children's school. Along the line, we got into a discussion and I just told him how the lady that owns the children has been patient with me regarding my children's school fees,that she hardly sends them home when there's school fees drive.

When we got to his destination,he asked me to park and follow him inside to come and take my money. I followed him and we went straight to the proprietress's office. He introduced himself as her husband and the lady asked if he knew me before and he said he didn't. She told the husband that three of my children were her students. The man told her that she should write off my kids' school fees. Without hesitation, she did and gave me the receipt.

The man told me that I should continue to be a good man no matter the situation I found myself in. He said my action alone encouraged him, that he was about to give me the sum of 50,000 naira but since I was yet to pay my children's school fees,he decided to help me and do so.

He also paid for my daughter's WAEC registration. I was filled with joy that day. It really pays to be good and to be different.I have decided to make those words he said to me my watchword every single day that passes by.

DAMIAN

"I came down to Abuja last year to stay with my elder brother. I came to Abuja so that I won't be a victim of the unreasonable massacre going on in the South East.

One day on my way back from work, I almost lost my life at a checkpoint. The policemen were going about their normal duty of stop and search and all of a sudden, gunshots were heard from opposite directions. All I could remember was that I felt a heavy push from behind and I fell into a nearby gutter. The shooting went on for more than 30 minutes and after sometime, everywhere was calm.

When I got out of the gutter, I saw dead bodies. Some people were injured and the police vans were on fire. I ran for my life. When I got home, everyone was worried because they were all calling my phone but it wasn't reachable. When my elder brother heard what happened he asked me to come down to Abuja.

Since I have been in this town, I would say that the fear of being hit by a stray bullet has completely disappeared from my thoughts. I have also overcome the trauma of that incident I experienced down there in the east.

The only challenge I'm having now is that I'm yet to get a job. I'm a handy person. My brother has also been looking out for jobs for me. Back then in the east, I used to work as a bus driver. I also did other minimal jobs.

I'm hopeful that soon, I will get a job and things will definitely turn around for me. I believe that once there is life, there is hope.

KIJEH

"I come from a very strict home. After my dad died, my mum became the disciplinarian. We were always careful with our actions in order not to incur our mother's wrath. But unfortunately, one of my sisters got pregnant outside wedlock. It was a devastating experience for my sister as my mum never wanted to have anything to do with her and the baby. They eventually reconciled after a long while.

When I met my boyfriend, I told him we were not going to be physically involved and he was okay with it. One day, I went to visit him and met a girl in the house. He told me that the girl had a fight with her boyfriend and ran to him for help since they were from the same tribe. Before I knew what was happening, the girl became pregnant for him and insisted he must marry her . At that point, I knew I had to leave the relationship even when he begged me to stay, that he would sort things out

Not long after I left, I met someone else and gave him the same condition. He accepted and we eventually got married. It was the fear of my mother that made me stick to my decision and I'm happy it paid off. "

EUNICE

When she was married to my son, we were not very close. That my son had never brought me peace. If not that I birthed him myself, I would have doubted if he was really my child. How a son will not care about his mother still surprises me. When he got married and kept his wife away from me, I was not surprised. Only God knows the lies he must have fed her. But even with his behavior, the wife tried to reach out once in a while. I guess he never really permitted it so she was not free to have a close relationship with me.

Years down the line, they got divorced. Knowing my son, I knew the fault would have been his. It is not easy living with someone like that. I lost contact with my daughter-in-law after the divorce and I felt that was the last I would see or hear of her and her children. But somehow, she found me and has been the one taking care of me.

Apart from my daughter who is also managing with her family, none of my other children, all men, care about me. It is my daughter-in-law that sends me money every month and also calls me regularly.

I cannot stop praying for her and thanking God for a woman like her. Other women would have forgotten about me especially since she is no longer married to my son but not this woman. What my children cannot do for their own mother, she is doing for me. I pray God continues to keep and reward her for all she has done for me."

JESSICA

"I was engaged to be married. Because we were in different states, I only visited him on holidays. One of the times I visited, I noticed how my fiancé was spending money unnecessarily. He was always going out with friends, partying, and clubbing. I called him to explain how uncomfortable I was with the way he was wasting money.

Meanwhile, his boss had entrusted his firm in his care. So, he was spending both his money and the commission he should have been remitting to his boss. When his boss found out what was happening, he was laid off. Things became rough and his friends deserted him.

On the other hand, I was not making much money. I had my family to cater for and also foot my bills. One day, he called me to ask for financial assistance. To be honest, I had no money because that period and month had not ended. I told him he should wait till month end, he became angry and said he was no longer interested in the relationship, that we should go our separate ways. I was shocked and heartbroken.

After our break-up, he met another girl and they eventually got married. Last month, he called to apologize for how badly he treated me, that we should reconnect. I asked him what he meant since he was already married. That was when he started complaining about his wife, saying how stubborn and bossy she was and that since he's a lawyer, the divorce process would not be a problem to him. I told him to go and patch things up with his wife. I cannot be a substitute. If I wasn't good for him then, what has changed now? He has made his choice, he should live with it."

OMUHA

"When I tell people I'd be needing 600,000 naira to upgrade my knowledge in a fashion academy and that I have tried borrowing for it, some look at me in a way that suggests I am not okay. Some go as far as saying my dreams are too lofty considering the fact that I do not have a kobo.

Others have suggested I look for a roadside tailor and continue from where I stopped. Why the roadside tailor is a bad idea is because I have been with them. Most of them only want maids without payment. My former boss from whom I learnt tailoring would give us clothes to wash including her husband's underwear. We would fetch water, not just for her but also for her friend. The time you would have used in learning would be spent on one errand or the other. The most annoying part is, if you should offend her, it's her husband that would pass the punishment.

There was a time he flogged an apprentice so badly she was hospitalized for 3 days and her phone screen also got shattered.

Her teaching style was very poor. She would just go on working without explanation until you ask. Even then, you'd have to ask repeatedly before she would explain.Sometimes if I got tired of asking, I would download videos on youtube and teach myself. Though her place was far from mine, I chose her because I heard she was among the best in the area.

After two years of being with her, I asked for my certificate and she requested 150,000 naira before giving it to me. I was not owing her for the training as I paid her fees even before commencing.

I offered 50,000 naira, but she refused and came down to 120,000 naira. Since I do not have that amount to pay her, I have left her alone.

I stay home and teach myself with YouTube videos and sometimes pay for online classes. I am a fashion lover and won't give up on my dreams of being a fashion designer someday. Until I get to the top, I am not giving up."

CHIZZY

I look at myself now and I'm grateful for where I am. Growing up wasn't easy emotionally. Financially, we were okay, at least my dad met our needs. Emotionally, the story was different;it was one quarrel or another and he transferred his anger on us. He would insult us and refuse to pay our fees until we apologize for what we don't even know.

Throughout our four years in the university, he never called to check up on us. He would just send money by month end and that would be all.

I met my husband when I was 20 years old and broken,but one thing I knew for sure was that he was a good man. I graduated and told my mom that one more year in that house would make me run mad.

I got married with a lot of flaws. I would shout at the smallest things; quarreled all the time. It was terrible. In all these, my husband never judged me, he doesn't even see them as bad. Instead, he has loved me continually. I tell my siblings that he's my reward for all the trauma I experienced as a child.

Though my husband doesn't have the luxury I enjoyed in my father's house, I even relocated from Abuja to a place some may call a village;still, I am happy with him. He pushes me, supports my business like his own and for that, I am a better person today.

For every pain you have ever felt, God is giving you happiness. Good men exist and I have one."

JOE

I got a better job offer and had to relocate here. The day I was to travel, I called one of my uncles who resides here to inform him and asked to stay with him till I get a place.

When I got here, I called to inform that I had arrived so he would send me the address to his house. He told me to wait as he would be coming to pick me up. I waited for hours, but he didn't show up. I called , but he rejected my calls. I became worried as I was stranded and had nowhere to go.

I had to go back to the establishment where I was offered a job. Luckily for me, I met a lady, narrated my ordeal to her, and she offered to help by getting one of her male friends to accommodate me. She became my very first friend in town and was always there for me.

One day, she came to me looking gloomy. I asked what the problem was and she said, "with all I've done for you, won't you ask my hand in marriage"? I was surprised! Just because she's been nice to me doesn't mean that I have to reciprocate the kind gesture by marrying her.

Last Christmas, she invited me to her family house. When we got there, she introduced me to her people as her husband-to-be. I was beyond embarrassed. I have tried talking to her but she is adamant. To crown it all, I have seen someone I love so much but with all this mess around me, I wouldn't want to drag her in until everything is resolved. I'm in a dilemma right now and don't know what to do. "

SONIA

"I grew up in a home where I was never loved by my dad. He treated me with hostility and so much hatred. He abused my mom, treated us like strangers until his death in 2012. My mom, who at the time, was a petty trader lost everything trying to save him from his illness. We were left with nothing after his death.Life became hard. I stopped going to school. Feeding was a problem for us.

One day, they sent for me from school telling me the proprietor wanted to see me. I went there and I was told to resume school immediately. I was happy. I graduated from secondary school by God's grace. I later learned computing which was partly funded by my pastor, but I couldn't graduate because we could not complete payment. After that, I started doing all sorts of menial jobs to assist my mom and siblings. Things were difficult for us but we never lost focus in God.

Sometime in 2017, when I was 18years old, I got a job in a hotel where I worked as a receptionist. The MD there offered to give me the sum of 600,000 naira if I would date him, but I refused because I made a convenant with God to not defile myself.

I am 24 now, I still can't further my education. Things are still hard, but I'm grateful to God for life. I have a musical career and I receive songs in dreams and visions. So far, I have over 30 songs written down and counting. I am hopeful that one day, God will remember my family and I will be able to achieve my dreams and wipe away tears from my mother's eyes."

AUGUSTA

"When I read stories about dads who sacrifice and love their kids, it baffles me a lot. I am from a family of 7 and the 1st daughter. I grew up seeing my dad beat my mum over everything and nothing. She never left even when I asked her to when I was 10. He would steal all she labored for. Each time any of us got sick and we asked for money to get medication, he would tell us to our face that he would make a coffin if we decide to die or he'd say, "go to the land of the dead if you do not see your mate, you can come back." Imagine your own father telling you this as a child.

I wanted to commit suicide several times,

but when I looked at my siblings and mom, I would have a rethink. I don't know why he hated us so much when he gave birth to us. I started taking care of my siblings when I was 16. I left home to try and see if things would change. I remember days I would sleep outside in the rain and getting raped just to raise money and pay my siblings' school fees.

Along the line, I got a skill and from the money I made from it, I enrolled in NOUN. My younger sister got a job as a secretary with her SSCE and also got enrolled in NOUN. Our last child is writing SSCE next year while the other two are taking JAMB this year. I do not have a dime presently and my father is busy sponsoring other people's children while we struggle to create paths for ourselves. My mom is presently doing nothing and my elder brother, the first son, is managing to survive.

I have been thinking of how we can come out of this suffering. It has stayed long enough. I will be 28 this year and all my life, I have been struggling. I really need someone to tell me it will be fine, that my dream to become a fashion designer will come to pass. I need someone to tell me my siblings will achieve their dreams and will succeed;that one day, we will look at the past and smile and everything will be alright."

DAMIAN

"I loved her and was trying my best to assist her the best way I could. There was hardly anything she asked for that I didn't give her. If it required me saving for it, I did and got it for her. I think it was because I felt I was trying. That was why I thought she would never cheat. We were in different towns, but we saw each other regularly because work always took me to her town. When I would go for those jobs with my colleagues, we were lodged in this particular hotel. I didn't know my so-called girlfriend was dating a senior colleague. Knowing I was there, she would still come to see him there and even spend the night. How she managed to do this for a long time without me catching her is still a shock to me. The most insulting part is that my colleagues, including the senior, knew she was my girlfriend. I can only imagine the jokes they were making behind my back.

The day I found out, I was going through her phone randomly. I had bought her a new phone and wanted to move her important files. It was the name that caught my attention and I decided to go through the WhatsApp messages. I read all their chats. I felt both anger and shame at what I discovered. When I confronted her, she denied at first but when I told her I read the chats, she started begging. She has been begging since. She has also sent others to beg but even if I want to forgive her, how can I continue dating her and have dignity before my colleagues? I regret not paying attention and I've promised myself to be more observant in my next relationship. "

OKWY

"My wife died 23 years ago. We had three kids together. They are all grown and staying on their own. My first child, who is my only daughter, lives in Norway with her husband while my first son and his family lives in Delta state. The last child recently relocated to Australia to further his studies. I'm all left alone in my house.

For the past 23 years since my wife passed, it was not easy for me. Raising these three children was difficult, but I kept on doing what I had to do as a father so that they won't feel the demise of their mother much. There were some nights I would just sit on my bed crying and asking God to bring back my wife. As time went by, I came to the full realization that she wouldn't come back here on earth. I believe she is over there in heaven watching over the kids and I.

Today, I can say that all my effort to train these children wasn't in vain because the life they are living now was the life my wife and I actually planned for them. I have been to Norway three times;whenever my daughter gives birth, my son-in-law makes sure I come over and spend some time with them over there.

Whenever I'm in Nigeria and I feel a bit bored or depressed, I travel to Delta State to stay with my son and the family. My last son was not always around,all he did was to make sure he made breakfast and lunch for me before leaving the house. Now that all of them are no longer with me, I feel very lonely and it makes me think so much about my wife. She was my best friend and my companion. My son in-law has asked me several times to relocate permanently with them over there, but I have told him I can't. I just prefer to be here. I walk around freely and I do go to visit my former colleagues now that we all are retired. The moments shared with them do give me hope and revive me instead of moving to a whole new country where I don't even have a friend. How do I start making friends at this age? Right now, I'm living my life and waiting for my own time to leave this earth because nobody lives forever. "

NGOZI

"I used to be slim before I got married. The birth of my children completely changed my body. I noticed I increased in size after the birth of my second child and when I spoke to my brother who happens to be our family doctor about it,he told me it's something I shouldn't be worried about, that the body of a woman changes once she begins to give birth. He reminded me that I used to say I wanted to put on weight when we were growing up and now that I have started adding, that I shouldn't start complaining that I need my old body size back. He advised that I shouldn't worry much, that once I finish giving birth, that I could snap back to my previous body size. Even though it wouldn't be exactly how I used to be.

My husband and I agreed that we were going to have only four children; be it boys or girls. God blessed us with three boys and a girl. My last child is fourteen years old. After I gave birth to him, I have strictly adhered to the meal plan my brother placed me on. I can tell you that for the past thirteen years, I have not gained weight nor increased in any part of my body. My body has remained the same. Most of my friends and classmates, whenever they see me, all say that I don't grow old nor have I changed in body size for the past thirteen years. I just tell them the simple secret which is eating healthy, staying away from some kinds of food and total abstinence from soda, and soft drinks.

It took lots of discipline before I could adapt to it. I had no choice because the weight gain was so drastic and rapid. For the benefit of my health, I had to quickly find a solution to it. I was lucky to have a brother who is an expert. What really made me have some concerns regarding the weight gain was that after the birth of my second child, I gained a lot of weight and I noticed I had some difficulties breathing. That was when I had to run to my brother for proper medical advice.

SOFIA

"17th October 2021 was the most tragic day of my life. It has broken me into pieces which I'm trying very hard to fix. I lost my dad to the cold hands of death after praying to God to keep him alive. I saw life leave his body gradually and he just laid so calmly.

His brothers got to the hospital an hour later to take his corpse to the mortuary. The first thing they demanded from me was my father's ATM card and his car keys. I couldn't answer as I was still crying and in shock. They searched my bag, removed his ATM card and car keys which he gave me to keep and also his promotion documents which he had asked me to bring for him to sign .They took them away including whatever else they felt was important.

After taking the corpse to the mortuary, we never saw our uncles again that period. No one called to check up on us. No one called to tell us about the burial arrangements. When we went to the village to find out the plan, the first thing they asked me was if I knew any other properties my father had anywhere. I was so disappointed. By then, they had already withdrawn huge amounts from my dad's account which we didn't know where it went .We heard about the burial dates and thought the ATM card would be returned to us but no one did.

They took everything plus the land documents, his clothes, the other house, and everything not minding that we were still in school, about to resume, and with bills to settle;rather, they made mockery of us that we won't get money to continue schooling.They also seized the key to the house we were supposed to stay in at the village to prepare for the burial. Still, we did our best. After the burial, I felt I had to be strong and do whatever I can to finish school which was my dad's last wish .

I have decided that no matter what, I'll study hard. Even if I have to work or do a business to see myself through school, I will do it ."

EMEKA

"I have come to understand that in life, there is nothing as important as family. Last year, I had an issue with someone regarding a job he gave me. After completing the work,he refused to pay me my balance. All. the effort I made for him to fulfill his own part of the bargain was not yielding any fruit.

One morning, I went to his house very early and he was about to go out. I asked him gently why he had refused to pay me my balance and why he also stopped taking my calls. He didn't give me any reasonable answer and I told him he won't go anywhere until he pays me my money because the boys that worked with me were on my neck for their money. Some even accused me of collecting the money and lying to them that I had not been paid.

Instead of this man to at least have some remorse,he just took his phone, made a call, and in less than five minutes, a police van arrived at his house. He told them to take me away and to not allow anyone to come and see me. This man was owing me the sum of 85,000 naira and had refused to pay but in my presence, he gave the policemen 20, 000 naira. I felt so sad and disappointed in the men we called the police. They didn't even bother to ask me what the problem was. They were just acting like zombies. One slapped me and pushed me inside the van and we drove off.

On getting to the station, I was already bleeding from my nostrils. One of them asked me to go and wash off the blood, but I refused. I told them to kill me and nothing would ever make me wash off that blood from my face. We got into the waiting room of the station, I saw a man who was neatly dressed in a police uniform and my mind told me he must be their boss. When he saw me, he asked who did that to me and I pointed out the particular one that slapped me. When he asked him the reason for doing that,this man lied that I resisted arrest and I tried to fight him. The boss now asked them why I was arrested, none of them could even say why. He told them since they didn't know why they arrested me, that they must be lying that I resisted arrest. When he asked me what happened, I narrated everything to him. He pleaded with me to not be offended. He asked me my name and it turned out that he was my father's cousin. He was enraged and ordered that those policemen that brought me to the station be detained. He asked another team to go and arrest that man. Luckily for me, as they were about to leave, the man was driving into the station. Immediately, I told the police boss and also added that he bribed them with 20,000 naira. The man was detained,and he also made an instant transfer of my money right in front of the police boss.

Assuming I did not meet my dad's cousin,those men would have roped me in with a serious and heavy crime which I didn't commit. Let's be very careful with these evil men disguised in police uniforms, they can do terrible things just because of money.

NKEM

We had stayed seven years in the marriage without a child. The doctors said we were fine and should be patient. I took drugs, I went native, still nothing changed. When it finally came, I didn't recognise it. I thought it was the usual malaria and typhoid. It never occurred to me to test for pregnancy probably because I did not get any of the common pregnancy symptoms like vomiting. I had even gone two months before I realized I had not seen my period for a long time. I didn't tell my husband. I wanted to be sure first.Those days were the happiest moments of my life.

As the pregnancy progressed, we found out I was pregnant with twins. Our joy knew no bounds. I practically lived in the hospital because we didn't want anything to go wrong. Delivery came and went well. I went home with my boy and girl as the happiest woman in the world.

They were three months old when my baby girl suddenly died. She wasn't sick, everything was fine. I think that was what made me angry. I went into depression. I forgot about my boy that was still alive. For months, I couldn't come off that feeling of loss. My husband tried but couldn't help me. I was angry at God, my husband and everyone around me.

Then one day, I heard that a colleague had died. I knew she had been looking for a child like me for a long time before God blessed her the previous year. It was like a bulb came on in my head. I started asking myself what I was doing. Why I was angry when I should be grateful that God kept me alive and still kept a child for me. I cried that day like I had never cried before.

My son is 3 years old now and whenever I think of how I abandoned him those months, I feel very guilty. I also feel bad that it took the death of someone to bring me back to my senses. In all, I am very grateful that God didn't look at my ingratitude and decide to take all he has given me.

ESANG

"Honestly, I have given it my best when it comes to looking for a job. I have submitted my resumé in so many organizations where I heard that there were openings,but I haven't been lucky. The last time I worked was during my NYSC program. I was supposed to have had a job last year but something terrible happened when I was invited for the interview. During the interview, the manager started making some sexual advances at me. She started by stroking my hair. I kept quiet because I felt she was admiring the hair. The next thing I noticed was that her hands were on my chest and was kind of trying to caress my breast. I jumped up immediately from the seat and asked her what that was for. She told me that if I wanted to get the job, that I had to be her girl. She said every other girl in the company did it with her and mine shouldn't be different. I just told her politely that my faith was against such acts and I walked out of the office. On my way out, I heard her say I should think about the salary and the benefits that would come with it and get back to her. The salary was good enough and with the benefits, I would be taking home 200,000 naira every month. I refused and didn't let that bother me. After that incident, I decided that I won't bother looking for a job because it's glaring that for you to get a well paying job, it's either by connection or play by the boss' rule.

I decided that before the middle of this year, I would see what I can do to raise money and start a small business because during my stay in the NYSC camp, I learnt how to make liquid soap,cake and pastries. While working in my PPA also, I learnt how to sew bedspreads,duvets, curtains and throw pillows. I have decided that I will put all these skills to good use. I plan to start off with sewing duvets,throw pillows and bedspreads. I have made contacts with people I would be buying materials from and we have all come to an agreement on how they would be supplying the materials needed. I have been doing some small jobs like cleaning of houses for people during weekends and also school runs for some parents so that I can be able to buy an industrial sewing machine and other equipment needed to start up. I'm also believing in God to help me accomplish my goal before my set time and I know he will do it for me. It's better I earn a living legitimately than getting myself involved with something I would regret in the nearest future.".-

EJIKE

"Whenever I hear people say behind every successful man there is a woman that made it possible,I concur with that statement. My life turned around 36 years ago when I met my wife. I used to have a small shop far back in the 80's where I was selling electronics and electrical equipment. My wife was an accountant before we got married. She was working with one of the financial institutions in the country then. Each time I went to their office to carry out a transaction,she would be the one to attend to me.Gradually, we became close friends. I proposed to her and she accepted to marry me.

Just within two years of our marriage, my wife helped me to push my business to a whole new level. She linked me up with companies that gave me contracts worth millions of naira. She was the person that advised me to travel out and purchase my goods directly from manufacturers. She also taught me that turnover in business is the secret of growing a successful business. We have four children. Two are doctors and they live abroad while the other two are here in Nigeria managing our business. Each time people ask me the secret of my success in business I just tell them it's my wife. She has been the pillar behind the successful years our marriage and business have enjoyed so far. I won't deny the fact that in marriages, there are ups and downs but when both of you understand each other very well and the love is there,it would be a smooth and healthy ride."

AUSTIN

"We had been together for one year. I went to her parents' house with my family members for an introduction on January 4th. She had been so nice and cool all the while we were still dating.I noticed something strange about her immediately after the introduction. She started talking back at me at every little mistake. She has become hostile; she doesn't want to hear that my friends came around or maybe that I was hanging out with my friends. Her attitude just changed completely. I have tried so hard to call her attention to most of these things but instead of taking corrections or making adjustments, she would flare up angrily.

I couldn't withstand that attitude for my sanity sake. I called her to come over last weekend for us to talk about it. She came around and I was trying to let her know the changes I noticed in her attitude. The next thing she said was that I should start learning how to live with it because that's who she's and that's what she wanted. Instantly, I had to tell her there that I wouldn't deal with that kind of attitude for the sake of my sanity. I told her it was over between us. I could no longer cope.

Honestly, I don't see any reason why one should pretend to be someone they want to have a relationship with. When they finally get married, they will now bring out their real character. This is one of the major reasons why many marriages are crashing these days. I promised myself that once I get married, I want to remain married till death do us part. I don't want to get married today and get divorced the next day. When we stop living in deceit, I think it would do some marriages and relationships a lot of good."-

FEGOR

"He is from Ghana and we have been together for seven years. He came to see my people and did what he could with the plan of completing it later. But because things were not easy for us, he has not been able to. We have been managing ourselves for years. Unfortunately, I have not been able to have a child after several miscarriages.

Three years ago when his mother died, we traveled together for the first time to see his people. That period, I supported him with everything I had. I even borrowed to add to what I had. Early last year, my own mother died. As the first daughter, there were certain things my husband and I were supposed to do. I don't have any brother, just my two younger sisters and I. I told him about it and he said we would sort it out when the time comes.

In December, he said he was traveling to his place. I was surprised because I knew we had been struggling and the transportation would be very high. I was thinking if he had such an amount of money, he would have saved it up to assist me. Two weeks after he got there, he called me saying that he didn't think he would be coming back. That there's nothing here for him and he would like to start up life again there. I took it as a joke but it turned out he was serious. It's been over a month since he left. I cannot reach him on the phone as I have no one's number there. The number he used in calling me does not go through.

It hurts me badly that he could do something like that. I am still hopeful he will return but if he doesn't, I will try my best to bury my mother and move on with my life. "

DAMILOLA

"My classmate opened this salon business for me. Way back when we were still in school, my dad was well to do. He provided everything we needed. He paid my friend's school fees from Jss 2 till he wrote his WAEC Exams. My dad also had the plan of sponsoring my friend through the university but that couldn't happen because death took my father away from us when we needed him the most. Things went from good to bad for us. It was even difficult for us to feed. My mother did her best, but we had to drop out of school to go and look for casual jobs to do so as to fend for ourselves.

As years passed by, my friend was lucky enough to have gotten someone who sponsored him through the university. I was surprised to see him in our house one evening after so many years. We hugged each other and had a long conversation. I told him how life has been treating us since we lost our dad. He asked what I was doing presently, I told him I was working in a salon as a barber. He said we should go and look for a shop in a choice area and furnish it with every necessary equipment needed to start up my own salon. At first, I thought he was joking until the next morning when we woke up, went straight to the market and bought everything we needed to set up the salon. The following day, we succeeded in renting a shop and he paid for everything.

After the shop was fully set up, he handed the keys over to me and told me that without my dad, he wouldn't have been who he was today and the only way he could return all the favor my dad did for him was to make life easier for me. It was when he left that the lawyer in charge of the property where my shop is brought a payment receipt that I found out he paid for three years rent. Tears ran down my cheeks. I called him to say thank you, but he said he should be the one thanking me for being a good friend that convinced my dad to be paying his fees when his mother couldn't afford to.

Today, I have two other branches and it was from the proceeds I got here I used in establishing those two. My friend has also been so supportive. Honestly, it pays to be good and kind to people whenever you have the opportunity to do so. You will always get the reward."

MEJI

"It was in 2019 I gave him money to get me a minibus. The plan was to use it for town service. Throughout that year, all I got was stories upon stories without seeing the bus.

In 2020, I feel very sick and was hospitalized for months. It was late in the year, while I was still in the hospital, the bus finally came. Since I couldn't drive it myself at the time, I told my brother to look for someone who would take it on hire purchase. I trusted him to know what to do, so I left him to sign the agreement with the person. I also gave him the 100,000 naira he requested for to get the vehicle registered.I was bedridden most of that year and 2021.

After six months of giving out the bus, I was informed it had packed up and the person had abandoned it. It was when I got better I went looking for it. I couldn't believe that was the bus I paid for. The engine had failed, the whole body was broken and most things inside damaged. I couldn't use it in that state and ended up spending 400,000 naira to get it fixed.

Recently, I went to renew the papers at the Road Safety Office. To my shock, they told me the vehicle papers had expired since 2013 and the plate number was not assigned to that vehicle. The solution was to do a fresh registration which would still cost me some money. I have told my brother and he keeps saying he will contact those who did the papers. To say I feel bad and disappointed is an understatement. I trusted him because I took him as a brother though we're not from the same parents. He is also knowledgeable in these things so I am surprised how the papers he claimed to have done in 2020 shows 2013 in the system. It can only mean no original papers were done and even the plate number was not new.

At this point, I am tired of the whole business. I just want to sell it off and have peace. Unfortunately, the offers I'm getting are not even close to half of the money I have spent on it. I had spent so much on my health and was hoping to start afresh with this bus but with the current situation of things, I am left with no hope."

MFONOBONG

"I married my husband when I was still in university. Before I graduated, I had given birth to three children already. My husband was nice and loving all along. The problem started after I had my fourth child. Honestly, I wish I could say exactly what I did wrong. He started keeping late nights and would flare up at the sound of my voice. All efforts to talk to him proved abortive. I became sad and unhappy, so I had to move out of the house with my children to clear my head.

Three months after I moved out, my husband brought in another woman who was already pregnant for him. I had no other choice than to file for a divorce.

Two of my children became very sick and were hospitalized. I called their dad to notify him of the situation. He sent some money and also came to visit them. After they were discharged, he insisted on taking them to his house which I allowed. While they were there, their father's concubine called me to come and carry my children, so that if anything happened to them, she wouldn't want to be held responsible. I recorded the conversation and forwarded it to my lawyer and my ex husband. My ex husband is now insisting on keeping the children with him. From the conversation I had with the lady, I know that my children are not safe. I'm working hand in hand with my lawyer to take custody of my children. I'm not denying him access to them. He can see them whenever he wants, but they have to be with me."

OLUSHOLA

"I have come to the point where I just give thanks to God for making me see another day. I used to have a shop where I was selling all kinds of drinks like wine,soft drinks,yogurts,water etc,but I lost it to demolition. I was newly married then,so it was a huge blow to me. I had to start from scratch. I relocated back to the village with my wife. At one point, some people started saying bad things about my wife, that she was the one that brought me bad luck. That she was the cause of my misfortunes. I just laughed at them. If only they lived in Abuja, they would have understood why it's nobody's fault but the government and the indigenes of the state that were to be blamed.

I ignored every complaint and tried to figure out a way to build up my life and business again. I told my wife not to worry, that things would get better and she shouldn't mind what people were saying ;nothing on earth would ever make me send her packing or see her as the cause of what happened to my business. I used the small money my younger brother gave me to start up this business of selling and hawking phone accessories. I started off with the sum of 60,000 naira. Gradually, I have been growing my capital. I have been planning on how I would start buying my goods directly from

Lagos where it would be a bit cheaper for me, since I would be getting it from the importers directly. I have contacted about four importers. They said I should at least start with the sum of 300,000 naira and they would give me goods worth 500,000 and above. So that when I sell, I balance them and collect another. I have been working hard towards raising the capital. My wife and brother have been so supportive. My wife is in the village. She does menial jobs and also sells farm produce she harvests from the farms. My plan is to establish myself once again, rent a house of my own because currently, I'm squatting with someone, then I would bring down my wife and the beautiful daughter God blessed us with back to Abuja. While I hawk my goods around, my wife would stay in the shop. To be honest, I make more sales when I move around. This time around by the grace of God, I would be very careful when I would want to rent a shop so that what happened before won't happen again.

I'm so grateful to God for the grace he gave me and also for helping me to provide for my family. Most of the people we were in the same line with have relocated and never returned. Some died due to the shock. My neighbor had a stroke and died. She was a widow with four kids and the business was the only source of income she used in taking care of her family. The bad part of this demolition is that they didn't allow us, the shop owners, to carry our goods, but they allowed all these scavengers to be packing our goods in our presence. Nothing hurts more than that. I thank God for my life and also for the opportunity to start up again. Someday, things will get better and that's my belief."

VIVIAN

"I searched for a job for two years after my NYSC. It wasn't easy. All the places I submitted my CV promised to get back to me, but they didn't. I was depressed and frustrated. The only thought that was crossing my mind then was: "After spending five years in the university and no job, is this how I want to build my future?"

One day, I decided to take a walk around my neighborhood and see if I could see any advert for job vacancies. On my way there, I saw a kiosk for sale. I approached the guy inside and enquired from him if he was the owner. He said yes that his visa just came out and he was raising money for his flight ticket so that he could travel. He was selling airtime and running a POS business there. I explained to him my plight and told him all I could afford then was 80,000 naira. At first he refused, but when he saw that I was serious, he said I should go and bring the money. I transferred the money to him immediately. He brought sales agreement documents which we both signed. He took his copy and gave me mine. After everything, he prayed for me and said that the grace that sustained him in this business would also sustain me. I said "Amen" to all his prayers.

This is my third year in this business and I don't feel like leaving it. I have opened two other branches from the proceeds I got from this one. I never knew that this business is quite lucrative. It has really helped me so much in my saving habit that's why I don't think I can leave the business to go do something else. I have learnt one thing in life;most of the things we look down on are definitely things that would later be our stepping stone to success."

MABEL

"We dated for about 7 months. As at when he was asking for my hand in marriage, there were two other men doing the same. I was confused because I was worried about making the wrong choice. I told my mother about it and she said she was going to take their names to a prophet to point out the right one. After a series of prayer and fasting, the prophet chose him. That was how we got married. The truth is, I didn't love him so much but I was willing to try since it was what God wanted.

After the marriage, I moved to the city where he lived. I would have loved to stay back a little because of work but he insisted I move and look for another job. The first week was fine but from the second week, we started having problems. He complained about everything I did—from cooking to house chores—nothing was ever good enough. I'd apologize and try to do better.

Two months into the marriage, he started coming back late. Then I noticed he was communicating with his ex-girlfriend. This was a girl he told me he had carried out the introduction rite on but broke up with her because she cheated. I still ignored it all hoping things would work out eventually.

Then on the 3rd month, he just packed his bags and left. When I called him, he said he didn't think the marriage would work so we should take a break to work things out. I was devastated. I attempted suicide twice, but I guess it isn't my time yet. I eventually moved back home to start my life again. It's been over a year, I am much better and hoping to find someone again."

JACOB

"I'm the fourth child of my family. While growing up as a kid, I was filled with so much energy that you would hardly see me sitting idle. My parents detected that trait and helped to put it into good use rather than engaging in unnecessary work. My mother, especially, helped me a lot. She would always make sure that I was in the kitchen and also made me engage in house chores. I started cooking at the age of ten. My mum had a local restaurant, my siblings and I were her staff. We would wake up as early as 4:00am to join her in preparing the food she would sell for the day before going to school. That was my daily routine as a kid. I got so used to it and it really helped in curbing my restlessness.

When we lost our dad, things became difficult for us. It wasn't easy for my mother to provide for us. We had to suggest selling food morning and night. The proceeds we would get from the morning sales would be strictly for house rent and minor expenses,while the proceeds from the night sales would be strictly for our school fees. That was how five of us were trained in school.

When I finished my secondary school, I had to work for two years to be able to raise money and enroll myself into an ICT school. After I finished my program,I worked with a telecommunication company.I also worked as a volunteer for two organizations all in the quest to build my CV. Many youths of today don't think of volunteering. I later relocated to Abuja for greener pastures. When I came, I saw that people in my neighborhood usually took their clothes to laundry shops,so while I was still looking for a job, I decided to be doing laundry for the meantime since I had been used to it as a kid. That was how I kick started my success journey. I finally got a Job with a PR company, Torch Blaze Media Consults, and I was also introduced to bitcoin by the CEO. I used my first salary to purchase bitcoin,which I left for three years before I sold it and used the proceeds to start up my life. I am married now. God has also blessed my wife and I with our own house. My success in life has been as a result of steady grind,honesty, loyalty and most importantly, staying focus on my set goal in life.``

FELICIA

"Before I got married, my husband was nice and caring. He would send me money even without me asking. If he saw me with unkempt hair, he'd immediately give me money to go make it so as to look good for him.

Few months into our marriage, he began to change. He doesn't care if I make my hair or not, use toiletries or even wear clothes. Fortunately for me, I had a little business so I was getting money I could use to take care of my needs. I always tried to look good for him yet nothing changed.

When I got pregnant, I started experiencing vaginal itching. I told my husband about it, but he said nothing. During ante-natal, I complained to the doctor and after running some tests, he said my husband should come with me for treatment. When I told him, he got upset saying that he is O+ hence not prone to infections. I tried explaining to him but all efforts proved abortive. He even said I must have gotten the infection from my sister's place where I had gone to visit earlier. I had spent only a few hours there and knowing how hygienic my sister is, I was sure I didn't get the infection from there.

After the delivery of my baby, I was given some antibiotics for the cut I had which also helped with the itching. After child birth, I suddenly lost the urge for sex. Again I told my husband about it and he said it was because of the delivery being my first time. I waited, hoping things would normalize, but it never did. Meanwhile, my husband would always plead that I let him and sometimes I did. That was how I got pregnant again. The itching also returned and anytime I tried talking to him about it, he'd get angry and we would end up quarreling. I decided to let the matter rest till after delivery. I was given drugs which helped to relieve the itch and burning sensation.

My marriage is three years and 7 months now and the infection is still untreated. I have been complaining, begging, crying about it, but my husband has paid deaf ears and keeps saying I'm the only one that knows where I got the infection forgetting that he married me a virgin.My first son has also gotten an infection which I believe was from the napkins he was using as a baby. I told my sister-in-law who is a nurse and after checking him, she prescribed some medications.I told my husband about it and he got furious. He said it was not possible for a child of two years to have a urinary tract infection but that if I insist, then I should take him to the hospital since I had enough to waste as he won't be giving me a penny for it. My baby and I have been managing the infection since then and enduring the itch.

My husband never takes anything seriously, especially our health. I always self-medicate my kids anytime they get sick, but this time around my kids have been having colds, coughs and catarrh for over 2 weeks and nothing I do or give to them has worked. Right now, I am confused and worried as my children, especially my first son, are losing weight and won't eat coupled with the infection the child is still battling. My husband insists it's normal for kids of that age but I know it's not.

I feel so sad that the man I married would change so much. I can no longer sustain the business because of my kids so I can't even afford taking them to the hospital. I just pray nothing happens to my kids before help comes."

CHIOMA

"At the age of 8, I was sent to live with someone in the city as a househelp. I lost my father when I was just six years old. My mother was a petty trader and the burden was much on her to take care of us. We were four in number and I was the second child. When she couldn't afford to provide for all of us, she had to succumb to the pressure of allowing my elder brother and I to go live with people as househelps.

The family I was living with had grown up kids;the youngest was about 15 years old. When they came to take me from my mother,they said a lot of sweet things. They even promised to train me up to university level. I was so excited because I thought I would be going back to school again.

When we finally went to the city,I stayed for one year and some months before I was enrolled in school. I felt really bad but I was happy because finally I got back to school. At my young age, I was made to do all the laundry in the house, clean the house and wash dishes. It wasn't easy on me but I kept on keeping on because I had a target which was to get properly educated since they were training me in school.

When I finished my secondary school education, I was so happy and excited,but my uncle's wife tried to cut short my happiness. I thank God for my uncle and his children who insisted that their parents must fulfill the promise they made that they would train me up to university level. My uncle's wife started getting suitors for me so that I would get married. She said I didn't need any education, that it's better for me to get married and help my family. The kids insisted that I must go to the university. They countered their mother by saying that it was a wrong decision for her to reward me with marriage after all I had gone through living with them for years. That was how I was able to go to the university and graduate.

I was in my final year when I met my husband. He was also in his finals. We graduated, stayed apart for a year due to our NYSC, and later got back together. We have been married for 13 years now and God has blessed us with three lovely kids. My husband and I are really working hard to make sure that we give our kids a proper education and also provide their needs so that they won't experience what we went through while growing up.

My advice to everyone out there is that we should always have patience no matter the situation we find ourselves in. Someday, we would be happy we did.

PETER

"I lived a rough life when I was in university. I was a member of a cult group. I did lots of terrible things. My plan was to become a medical doctor, but because of my rugged lifestyle, I fell out woefully. In my 300 level, I had to switch over to Engineering.

While I was in school, I had a girlfriend who was from a wealthy home. She knew about my way of life but chose to stay with me. She became pregnant for me. I insisted she abort it but she refused. She took the money I gave to her and ran off to the village to stay with her grandmother until she delivered. When her dad heard about it, he accused me of raping his daughter and arrested me. My family fought for my release.After I was released, the baby was given to me as the girl's family didn't want to keep her. My family, on the other hand, told me to carry my cross. I had no other choice than to cater for my baby all alone. I took her everywhere I went. She became a very special part of my life.

My baby mama is married to another man . I'm so happy she didn't terminate the pregnancy. That's why anytime she calls to ask for anything, I don't hold back from assisting her. "

NNEKA

"We met on Facebook and almost immediately, he told me he was looking for a wife and would like to marry me. I told him to calm down so we could get to know each other first. That was how we became friends and started talking regularly. We lived in different states and over time, he started inviting me to visit him. Considering everything going on in the country, I was afraid to make such visits and I told him so. Besides, my work wasn't giving me enough time. He always got angry each time I turned down his invitation. I saw it as a red flag. We finally met when work took me to the state, but I didn't spend the night.

The second red flag was the fact that he was always telling bogus stories of his wealth and properties and would even send pictures. Whether they were true or not, I couldn't tell, but the fact that he always had to brag about it was a turn off for me. I finally had an opportunity to visit him in December. My sister lives in the same town, and I had gone to deliver something to her. I was supposed to spend only a night there. When I got to his house, he told me he had a function to attend with his bosses and since I was already there, I should join them. I wasn't dressed for it but decided to oblige him so he doesn't get offended.

At the function, there was plenty to eat and drink and we had our fill. My plan was to get to his house, stay a while and then leave for my sister's place. Unfortunately, it was raining heavily and I had to stay longer. At one point, he stopped contributing to our gist and concentrated on his phone. I could notice he was angry because I refused to get comfortable by taking off my clothes as he suggested or spend the night. I got bored and uncomfortable and decided to leave under the rain since it was getting late too. I had expected he would go drop me off but he simply told me goodbye without even leaving his seat.

When I got to my sister's house, I sent him a text to let him know I arrived safely. What I got was a long message on WhatsApp telling me how I was proud and not a good wife material. That we came back to his house and I couldn't go to the kitchen to prepare something like a good wife would do. He said my education had gotten into my head and if I didn't humble myself, no man would marry me. I just took it that he was looking for an excuse to quarrel or cut me off so I ignored him. It's been three weeks since then and we haven't spoken to each other. I am just happy I didn't fall into his trap of a marriage,only God knows what he would have turned me into."

EFE

"Honestly as a man, you need to be up and doing your responsibilities in taking care of your family. I have been working as a waiter and also as a night security guard to meet up with my responsibilities as a man. I have really learnt a lot in the line of my duty. I have learnt that the best way that you can live and interact peacefully with humans is to be humble and loyal. Nothing beats humility and loyalty while dealing with humans.

I earn a total of 40,000 naira from my two jobs and plan my budget around the amount and also save from it. Most of my colleagues are always surprised whenever they come to me to borrow money and pay back when they receive their salary. With my responsibilities as a family man, it still amazes them how possible it is for me to still save from my salary. I only tell those who care to know what the secret is;customers give me tips due to how I attend to them and I also use my remaining spare time to work as a security guard at night. In all, I only have five hours of sleep for myself every day and also, I deprive myself of some unnecessary things that are not my immediate wants. All this sacrifice is just to meet up with my responsibilities as a man. I am also looking forward to starting up a small business for myself;an outdoor cafeteria where I would be selling food and drinks. I have an empty space already. All I'm working towards it now is to get the electronics I need and utensils. It is my set goal for the year 2022. I know I will definitely achieve it.

CYNTHIA

"He was the one that got me the job so when he said we should open a joint account, I didn't object. This was even before I got my first pay. Immediately the pay came, he asked me to transfer all the money into the joint account. From there, he gave me a small amount to get something for myself. We were both civil servants, but my pay was higher than his.

As the children grew older, the expenses increased. They went to good schools and we had a relatively good life. Most of these were financed by my salary. Every penny I got from work;bonuses, raises, any money at all, went straight into the account. In fact, my husband monitored my salary to the point that if there was any delay, he'd start disturbing me about it and even doubt if I say I hadn't received it.

They gave us a car loan one time, I transferred it all to the joint account and didn't get the car. Even before the car loan, if I had wanted to buy a car, I would have bought one but my husband said one car was enough for us. He would drop me off at work and come pick me after work. My colleagues always teased me on how we were inseparable, they didn't know it was my husband's idea and I really would have loved a car of my own. There were times I'd need to attend a function and had to join someone else. It was embarrassing especially if it's a work function because everyone had a car except me.

One day, a junior colleague asked me what I did with my own car loan when even she who got a lesser amount was able to get a car. I felt the insult deeply and could only imagine the gossip that had been going around. I couldn't get good clothes or anything nice for myself because for every money I asked for, I must give an explanation for it and it's only when my husband was satisfied that I'd get it. If my children needed anything, they would go to their father, even when they came to me, I'd still direct them to their father because he controlled the account. The worst of it is that I couldn't give my own family money. If my mother or any family member should ask for help and I mentioned it to my husband, he would rather send the money himself and receive the thanks than let me have access to it.

I had endured this for too long but just did not know how to get out of it. What surprised me the most was how he always knew when I got any extra payment. Little did I know that a colleague of mine, another lady, was the one giving him the information. One time we received a bonus and because I needed money to take care of something, I kept a part of it. To my shock, my husband told me I didn't transfer the full amount. He even mentioned the actual amount I was paid. I admitted I took out a part of the money. This man started threatening fire and brimstone if I didn't transfer the rest. That was when I knew there would be no getting out of the situation if I didn't get out of the marriage. How could someone threaten to kill me over my own money?

Twelve years was a long time to endure all I did and I felt I had had enough. I first of all told my mother about it and she was shocked and also angry. I kept it to myself all these years. I told my children too and they were equally surprised because they always thought their father earned more and didn't know most of our finances came from me. While I think of how to sort my children out, I have moved out of the house. Thankfully, they are in the University and may not need to go back to the house if the worst happens. I have told him I cannot do this anymore. It is left for him to take it or let me go."

IFEOMA

"A friend got a job for my husband so we had to move from the village to the city. Though the salary wasn't much, it was better than life in the village. We were happy with the little we had until one fateful day after I had my set of twins, my husband disappeared and abandoned us with nothing. I was devastated and confused at the same time because I had no source of income. Our rent was due for renewal and I had no money.

One day, a friend visited and I narrated my plight to her. She told me there was a woman in her church who could help with my accommodation. When the lady visited, she said she had a space in her compound and she would erect a zinc house for me to manage till I got something better. She did as she said and I moved in with my children.

With money I got from people, I started selling abacha. I had to hawk from street to street in order to sell so as to provide food for my family. I hawked on the streets for two years and emaciated so much I became a scarecrow. Sometimes I would look at myself in the mirror and cry my eyes out.

Gradually, I saved up and started a food business. So far, the business is doing well. My children are now in their teenage years. I'm glad God brought good people into my life. If it wasn't for them, I sincerely don't know what would have become of me and my children."

UJU

"At the beginning of 2021, I was earning 40,000 naira. It was a very poor amount considering my professional qualifications, but I had been on that pay for over three years. I started work after NYSC without pay, then I got a job that paid 40,000 naira and later moved to another for the same pay, but with better working conditions. It was embarrassing earning that kind of amount, especially when I look at my mates in school and how much they were earning. I was hopeful that someday, something better would come. To augment my income, I took on another side job, it wasn't easy but the extra pay helped.

In February, the company where I worked got a contract and because I'd be handling most of it, my pay was increased by over 100%. I bargained for more but even what I got was a lot compared to what I had been earning for a long time. I was happy and excited. I saw it as a breakthrough for the year, little did I know that God had more in store.

Sometime in June, a friend sent me a job advert. I wasn't very keen on applying because I felt I was now in a better place and was also tired of applying to jobs without success. At a point, I started thinking they didn't even read my CV because I rarely got called for an interview. In the end, I applied. Few weeks later, I was invited for an exam. It was tough and I didn't think I did well. A week after that, I was invited for an oral interview. After that, I still attended a virtual interview. By this time, I was already frustrated with the whole process but a few friends I told about it kept encouraging me.

Long story short, I got the job. Out of over 200 persons that sat for the exams and ten that attended the interview, I made it to the top two they took. When I got my appointment letter and saw the remuneration, I couldn't believe it. I had expected something big knowing the organization but never in my wildest imagination did I expect what I saw. I went hundreds of percent above where I was. It was like going from grass to grace. In a twinkling of an eye, my life changed. It wasn't only about the money, but the other benefits and the opportunity to work for an organization like that.

What excites me the most is that I got the job on merit 100%. Other than God's hands in it, it was my hard work that paid off. I see people reject jobs because of low pay. What they do not know is that the low pay job can give them the experience they need for the bigger job and when the time comes for that big job, nothing will stop it.``

HENRY

"It was when I traveled overseas that I discovered why God blessed white people more than other races. White people are so humble. They have human feelings. They are the richest race in the world. Statistics show that the richest people in the world are white people. You do not see them all over social media like other races. They invented Social media, they built Planes, cars, Ships, cellphones, etc. They also invented electricity. Everything we use as human beings literally has their imprint, yet, they do not brag as one would expect.

For instance, the whites built in the horns in cars, but you hardly see them use it indiscriminately irrespective of where they are going. I know a very wealthy man in the city where I live,my boss' landlord. As at 2006, he was worth $16million with over 88 houses in my city yet this man drives only one pickup truck and each time he comes to take his rent, once received, he will say "Thank you sir." The pickup truck I I knew him with since 8 years ago is still what he drives today. I couldn't help comparing him to my race. In Nigeria here, you will find someone of that status moving about with armed men.

Something else that interests me about the whites is their elections. Everything just goes peacefully. Then about their integrity, one day I got sick and went for a medical check up. I paid $74 for laboratory tests and after some weeks, the headquarter of the laboratory refunded me $18 with an apology letter, saying I was overcharged. That totally blew me away as that can never happen in my country. We really have a lot to learn from the whites and top on the list is humility. If we humble ourselves, we will achieve greater things.``

AMINU

"I will be 55 years old on the 29th of this month. My first son will be 20 the same day. We both share the same birthday and he is in his final year in the university. I'm a devout Muslim, but my boss is a Christian from the east. I have been working with him for the past 30 years, way back when I was still a bachelor. My boss has really impacted my life so much. Asides paying my salary,he and his family have been the ones taking care of my three children and their education.

When I was about to get married, my boss and his wife called me into their sitting room. He advised me that he knew that my religion permits me to have more than one wife, but if I could at least take his advice, I should just get married to who I love and build my life with that one person that I would never regret. I'm from a polygamous family and I know how difficult it was for my siblings and I because our mother was the third wife and we were younger than all our step-siblings. I took his advice and I can tell you that I have never regretted any bit of it. My wife and I also decided to have only three children and we would do our best to make sure we give them the best out of life. My boss has really been helpful in helping our kids realize their dreams. This would be the 10th time my family and I would be celebrating the Christmas holiday with my boss and his family in the east. I just came to the market to buy boxes and clothes for my family.

Honestly, I wish there were more people that could look beyond religion and ethnicity and let love lead;we would all live in peace. I pray and hope that such a time would come to pass in my lifetime. If you see my kids, it's only when they tell you their names that you would believe they are not Igbo. It gives me joy that they are able to mix up with people from different ethnicities and religions.

I wish all Christians around the world a Merry Christmas and Happy New year in advance. As we celebrate, let's also remember the reason for the season."

DEBBY

"I am twenty one years old, the second child in a family of four girls. When things were going well for us, my sister was enrolled into the School of Nursing while I had dreams of studying Law. We lived in Jos with our parents until May last year when my dad decided to send my mom and us away because she didn't have a male child. The quarrel about a male child had been going on quietly for a long time until my elder sister wanted to go to school and he refused to sponsor her. Our maternal uncle had to step in to help. Living with my mom and sisters was really difficult. Though my mum was trying her best to provide for us, I started looking for a job so as to save something while waiting for my sister to finish school before starting mine.

In the course of my job hunt, a male friend told me to come over to Abuja to work in a restaurant close to where he works. Unfortunately, by the time I got to Abuja, the job was no longer available and I had to stay with him as he promised to help look for another job for me. One fateful night, he forcefully had sex with me even when he had never made any advances at me. I was pained, but couldn't leave. It later turned out to be a daily demand from him. One day I asked him about the job, he got so angry he beat me up. I had no choice but to keep shut about it as I had no money on me either.

At the end of the month, I discovered I did not see my period. When I informed him, he casually said I should abort. I felt so bad about it and informed a friend who advised me to take the money and come live with her. That was how I left his house.

It was after I had moved in with my friend I discovered she was into prostitution. She advised me to get an abortion and come join her. While I was still debating on what to do, my boyfriend asked me to come visit him. I was worried he'd discover the pregnancy, but my friend asked me to go so I can put the responsibility on him.

Two weeks into my stay with him, I informed him I wanted to leave. He asked that I let the matter be till he returned from work. When he came back, he sat me down to talk. He told me he had read my chats with my friend about my condition and he understood everything. He said he'd look after me even with how bad things had gone. I was surprised, speechless and doubtful, but he assured me he was genuine and won't change.

I decided to give it some time and see truly if he'd follow through with what he said. Along the line, I noticed that things were not going that well for him and I suspected he had gotten tired of me. I noticed he wasn't going to work again and when I asked, he said he lost the job, but was trying his best to find another.

At this point, I am confused about my life. I understand that I got into all this trouble just because I wanted to find something clean and reasonable to do, but it is also my fault that I am suffering today. It has been almost three months that we are together and he actually hasn't changed, but things are not alright for us even though he hides it a lot and people around have started noticing my condition and think he is responsible.

I know I should be ashamed of myself for getting into such a problem and having to write about it, but I only wish things could get a little better so I will deliver safely and face my challenges of looking after my child and pursuing my education."

VICTOR

"My dad left the village for the city in search of greener pastures. We were living in a mud house then. One day, a heavy rain fell and the house collapsed. Thank God it happened when no one was at home.

Meanwhile, I have two uncles who have built houses in the same vicinity. One of them offered us a room, but my mum declined the offer because she was not in a good relationship with my uncle and his wife. She rather chose to go back to her parents' house which was not too far from my father's family compound. I told my mum that I was not going with her. So, I had to accept the offer from my uncle. I moved in with him. He employed me to work in his mill. He was feeding me and also paying my school fees.

One day, when I returned from school, his wife rushed into my room and started screaming, calling me a thief. I was shocked. When my uncle came back, she told him I stole her gallon of palm oil. Of course my uncle believed her. When I reported the matter to my mum, she was angry and had to confront my uncle and his wife which escalated and led to a fight.

After I finished writing my SSCE, I told my uncle that I would no longer stay with him. That was how I left the village to the city to hustle. Luckily for me, I got a job almost immediately. Now I've started molding blocks at home. Even if it's two rooms, at least I'll have a house to lay my head on each time I travel to the village."

RAPHEAL

"My dad lost his job when I was still in Junior Secondary School. So, my mum took up the responsibility of catering for the whole family. She was just a petty trader. Because she was not making enough money from the business, she had to switch over to roasting plantain (bole business). She worked so hard to provide all our needs. Meanwhile, my dad had given up on the search for a new job. What pained me most was the fact that he never allowed my mum to rest. He was always embarrassing and abusing her at the slightest provocation. My siblings and I became so scared of him. We dared not eat when he had not eaten. It was like he never wanted us to be happy.

My mum endured so much abuse from my dad. In fact, when I was in SSS 3, I told my mum to go home to her people that we would fend for ourselves, but she refused. After I graduated from secondary school, I started working as a sales boy. I saved up enough money and was able to purchase a JAMB form. I wrote the exam, passed and was offered admission. With my mum's help, I was able to pay my year one fees.

Unfortunately, my mum died when I was in my second semester. At that point, I wanted to give up. She was my strength and pillar. I had to have a rethink. I knew my mum would not be happy if I gave up so I continued. It wasn't easy. I did a lot of menial jobs just to get money to foot my school bills.

My dad on the other hand never cared if my siblings and I existed. My mum's family had to step in to take care of my younger ones. Sometimes, I squatted with friends since the house was no longer conducive for me. Today, I'm a graduate. I'm glad I didn't give up. In all, I give God the glory. I wish my mum was still alive to see me get to this point."

DORCAS

"I still remember how I took pen and paper and wrote down all I wanted to achieve before the end of the year. Out of the seven things I wrote, I have been able to achieve only two and five are yet to be achieved. On the 1st of December when I brought out my diary to check how far I have gone with achieving my set goals for the year;I just smiled, looked up to the sky, thanked God for the gift of life and also for giving me good health. I experienced so many challenges this year. I saw some of my mates that died this year. I saw people who in just a day lost all they had been toiling for. When these few thoughts crossed my mind while I was still worried that I couldn't achieve my set goals, I had nothing to say but to thank God for keeping me alive. I know the year has not ended yet, but one thing I believe is that as long as there is life, there is hope and as long as I keep on working hard, I know that I will definitely achieve all that I desire.

This year has really taught me so many things and at the same time, it has also been a beautiful year because it's the year I made my first 500,000 naira and also entered an airplane for the first time in my life. I emerged as the best staff in my company and the star prize was 500,000. The company paid for my flight ticket to and fro the headquarters in Lagos where I was presented with my cash prize alongside other winners from different branches. That alone was a big win for me. I'm keeping my hope alive that I will achieve all that I wished for even if it's not this year, but I believe all will come to fulfillment

CALISTA

"As a little girl, life was beautiful. My dad provided all that I needed to be comfortable in life. Things became rough when he lost his job and we had to move to a different city. In the process, I met a missionary family who hired me as a maid. I was paid based on the number of hours I worked. From the accrued savings, I was able to buy my toiletries and pay for my workbooks in school.

When the missionary family had to travel for their long vacation, I was referred to another missionary family and some rich Nigerian families too. I worked for these families, saved up enough money and started a recharge card and bole business with the help of my friend who is now my husband. Since I was making enough money, the idea of furthering my education after secondary school was no longer in the picture. My dad persuaded me and insisted I buy a JAMB form. Though I was reluctant, I just had to please my dad. My dad desperately wanted to have a graduate in the house. I bought the form, sat for the exam and passed. I was offered admission into one of the universities in the country, with a course different from what I chose. I really wanted to study Mechanical engineering, but I was offered petroleum Engineering. I wanted to forfeit the admission, but my dad would not allow it. That was how I ended up studying Petroleum Engineering.

While in school, things were rough for me. I was solely fending for myself and also assisting my family. At one point, I was angry with my dad for insisting that I go to school when he didn't have the money to support me.With my recharge card, bole business, and the money I got from the families I worked for, I was able to pay my fees.

I am glad I listened to my dad. Today, I am a certified Petroleum engineer with a Masters Degree and Phd in view. "

ESE

"I met a girl I had the intention of getting married to in the future. When I met her, she had just graduated from secondary school. I was in my early twenties, working as a manager in one of my uncle's filing stations. When I told her my plans, she accepted, but insisted on becoming a university graduate before settling down. I was ready to shoulder the responsibility as she was from a poor background and I knew her parents could not afford the expenses. Before she embarked on her academic pursuit, I met with her parents, told them my plans and they accepted.

When she gained admission, I was there for her financially and supported her every step of the way. I was also fending for her parents. When she finally graduated, I started making plans of making our union official, but she told me that she was no longer interested in me. When I asked her why, she said she could not marry an illiterate like me. I was shocked. I went to her parents, but immediately they saw me, they chased me away. I was beyond broken. At that moment, I was confused and didn't know what to do. In fact, what pained me the most was the comment she made. She said, "when you finally marry and bear children, I'll train one of them so it won't look like you wasted your money on me." This is pure wickedness. But I'm glad I found love at last. Today, I'm happily married with two beautiful children. "

YEMI

"I have a friend whom I've been friends with for about ten years right from the beginning of our University days. We constantly reminded each other while we were in school that we wouldn't miss each other's wedding for anything. Her wedding took place a few months ago and I met the husband for the first time though I had known him for a while because she always spoke about him, and also told him about me.

I was in the west while the wedding was to take place in the South. I had to travel down to the South for the wedding;bought the Asoebi, new shoes and made new hair despite not having enough money at that time. I felt our friendship was worth the sacrifice. I wanted to get her a gift but after making those expenses, I didn't have money left for it. Rather than go empty handed, I decided to wrap a souvenir I got from a burial party I had attended some months back and also added a smaller gift to it.

I wrapped and presented the gifts to her and was also given a souvenir in return.

Few days after the weddIng, she called to tell me she saw the gift I bought for them and that she didn't expect me to get that kind of gift for her. She said her husband was so angry he destroyed them immediately. The husband no longer wants to hear my name and assumes I wasn't happy for them, hence the reason I brought a gift with a deceased person's picture.

I explained that I didn't mean any harm and apologized since it hurt them. I even told her to pass the phone to her husband so I could explain and apologize to him but she said there was no need for that. Since then, she stopped calling and I also don't feel the urge to call her like I used to. I feel she and her husband already made their conclusions about me. I also told her they were reading too much meaning into it and she said it would have been better if I didn't bring any gift at all. I feel bad because our friendship of over ten years is gradually fading away. What should I have done better? If I had known my gift would lead to something like this, I wouldn't have added them. I have learnt from what happened and I'll have to let it go. "

OSHOKS

"Presently, I can beat my chest and say that I'm the most frustrated Nigerian as it stands now. I live and work in Germany. I came back to Nigeria three months ago to facilitate the process of moving back to my base with my wife and three kids. I already had all the necessary documents needed for this process, but guess what has kept me back for three months and slowed down all the process;the Nigerian corrupt system.

The first week I arrived in Nigeria, I went with my family to immigration to get their passport. I was asked to get them enrolled on NIMC and get their NIN. We enrolled for NIN and we were told it would take 5-7 working days to be uploaded on the immigration website. The first 7 working days passed and there was no result from NIMC and no data was transmitted to immigration database.

Two weeks ago, we succeeded in getting the NIN number and went back to immigration office and we were told that NIMC is yet to upload the data on their website. I was completely shocked and at the same time disappointed. How can they allocate huge amounts of money to all these organizations and at the end of the day, they will end up giving you flimsy excuses for their failure and incompetence? The way I have closely monitored all their activities, I can confidently tell you that this nation is not anywhere near ready to go into digitalisation. I think they should completely stick to what works for them, which is the analog way. I thought this country would have gotten better than when I left but I'm surprised that it has even gotten worse than before. The only way I think this country would get better is to collapse the present structure and get qualified and capable hands that can handle the affairs of this nation. Honestly, I respect those that have the courage to endure all this mess and still provide for their family. To be honest, I don't see any future for my kids in this country with the way things are structured in this country."

FRANCA

"He has a daughter, I also have one. I felt that was a good thing as his daughter who is already an adult would act as the older sibling to my teenage daughter. I felt we would be able to have a happy family with both of us coming together to make it work. So we started dating. The relationship would have been good but for his daughter. Every single thing he did, he said, was for his daughter. Everything he said had a way of including the daughter. We couldn't have a conversation without him trying to make it about his daughter and compare every other lady to her. I didn't see it as a big deal at first, but when he started seeking permission from her and giving up our time together for her, I decided to call his attention to it.

You cannot be in a relationship with the intention of marriage and still place your daughter above the person. He didn't see anything wrong with what he's doing. He even said I didn't like his daughter. I had to let the relationship go. As much as I want him to have a good relationship with his child, that kind of friction between us will cause issues in the marriage. I have had my share of love and marriage and I can do without it at this age."

DORCAS

"I dated my husband for 7 years before he finally proposed to me. We got married a year after the proposal. I was already working and doing very well for myself. When I told my husband that I would like to acquire a Masters Degree, he told me to hold on. I had the money to take care of my expenses, but my husband told me to rather assist him in getting his Masters first since I was earning more than him. I accepted.

Two years later, I became pregnant. We were so excited. Our joy was cut short when I lost the pregnancy due to high blood pressure. It became a recurring situation that each time I became pregnant, my blood pressure would rise uncontrollably which made it impossible for the fetus to survive. My husband was always around giving me moral support.

One day, a very close friend visited. Before she came, she told me that she had something very important she would like to discuss with me. When she came, she told me that my husband was seeing another woman. I found it difficult to believe her and decided to carry out my own investigation. I found out the truth, confronted my husband, but he denied it.

One of the days he told me he was going to work outside the state and that he would be away for three days, I knew he was lying. True to my instinct, my husband was actually going to another woman's house. I decided to pack all his things to where he was with the other woman and that was the end of the marriage.

After our marriage ended, I decided to adopt two children. I was able to further my education up to Ph.D level. Today, I am a senior lecturer in one of the universities and a proud grandmother too.

Ladies, your life is very important. There are a lot of things you can achieve in life. Don't allow anyone to tie you down."

NNANNA

"We were elementary school classmates back in the 90s. One year and some months after I traveled abroad, we reconnected on Facebook. I asked her if she was in a relationship and she said no, but actually she was in a relationship then. We began talking and as at that time, I was still struggling to get on my feet. We spoke about marriage, but I also let her know I didn't have a good footing yet where I was. Later on, she started pressuring me with the issue of marriage and I had no option than to stop talking to her because of the pressure I was also facing abroad.

Few months after I stopped talking to her, she got married to the man she was dating in school. When I saw the marriage pictures on Facebook, I congratulated her.

A year later, she lost her pregnancy which I also got to know from her post on Facebook and consoled her. When she finally gave birth, I congratulated her. I got to know they were down financially and she was the one footing the bills with her job after the husband lost his. Even after the husband got another job, she was still bearing the burden because he didn't pay much.

She became pregnant again and needed to undergo a Cesarean Section. She came to me asking for assistance which I readily gave. Sometime after that, her husband got an opportunity to go work abroad and he left. Coincidentally, I was to visit home too that period and told her about it. She was excited and asked that I visit her. I told her that won't be right as we do not know how we would react towards each other and end up doing something we'd regret.

After I had gone and returned without visiting her, she became angry with me. The next time I went home, I decided not to inform her. I only told her after I had gone back and still gave her reasons why it was unwise for us to meet.

That was when she began to insult me with all manner of words. I reminded her of when she needed help to pay hospital bills and I assisted her. After her insults, I stopped talking to her. She later came back to apologize, but I quickly blocked her. She has sent me friend requests on Facebook several times, but I haven't accepted. I am very happy that she has joined her husband abroad. She sent me a friend request again some days back and I still didn't accept and never will. All I do is wish her the best. "

TONY

"I am from a poor background. I won't blame my parents because I do not know how life was for them and how they were able to overcome depression and not give up. My father had me at his old age and I think that contributed to what I am facing today. He struggled hard to see us through primary and secondary school.

My elder brother was lucky enough to get a job after secondary school from which he made some savings and is now running his HND programme in the North. I was not so lucky but decided to join my father in his farming.

In 2016, I single handedly cultivated 1500 hectares of a cassava and maize farm which provided the funds I used for my registration when I gained admission into a Federal College of Education. I had earlier sold my phone to purchase a JAMB form. My plan had been to go to a university, but my fear was that I had no one to sponsor me. Unfortunately, the first time I gained admission, I had to forfeit it because I couldn't pay the school fees. In 2017 when I gained admission into the Federal college, I was still managing the small farm and anytime I went home for holiday, I cultivated something.

In school, I was made a class representative and was also active in the Student Union Government. To the glory of God, I graduated excellently a few months ago without any carry over, despite the 85 courses offered during my 3yrs programme. I have the intention to further my education, but no money at the moment. I have been thinking of farming which I already know how to do but this time,I do not want to do it manually. In the course of my three years programme, I had lung issues due to the cold, smoke and dusty particles I had to deal with while farming. My lungs have been adversely affected since then. Some say it's pneumonia, but I do not want to accept it and in spite of the health challenges it brings, I believe I will overcome it someday. It is because I do not want to engage in farming manually and endanger my health further.

I love being a farmer. I remember those times I used to give people maize while returning from the farm. I love to see the happiness and gratitude written all over their faces. I do not like seeing people go hungry. I believe I can help more through farming, but I still need support and advice on how to go about it. About furthering my education, there are several reasons I'd like to, one of which is that my father was insulted and ridiculed because of his situation. I want to prove to those people that a black pot can produce white pap."

OYEKWE

"When he called early this year, the first thing I asked him was if he was suffering from a terminal disease. He didn't understand why I would ask him that so I explained further. The only reason an estranged husband would want to reconnect with you is when he is at the verge of death. Either he is looking for a nurse to take care of him or he wants to seek forgiveness for his sins.

Our last child was just three, the others were five and eight. I cannot say I was the perfect wife, but I know I tried. I wanted it to work, if not for me, at least for the children. His complaint was that I was pursuing my career too much. I should stay home more and look after the kids. It wasn't like I was neglecting my duties at home. I was still the one who did all the cooking. The help I had only assisted and took care of the kids in my absence. I was bringing in the major part of the money in the house, yet my husband wanted me to leave the job or get one that would be less demanding of my time. He started using it as an excuse to stay out late. He would even travel and stay weeks for no good reason. I ignored it. Even when I started getting rumors of his philandering, I still looked the other way.

It was when he started being abusive though not physically, I had to ask myself serious questions. If it was just between us, I wouldn't have minded, but to abuse me at every opportunity and before any and everyone was something I couldn't take. Even my children felt it and I didn't want them experiencing that at all.

I was still debating whether I should endure or leave, when he decided to leave. No reason was given, no plan for the children, he just traveled as usual and never came back to the house. I took it as God's plan, turned to my children and put in everything. I had to make sure they did not lack. Over the years, he made feeble attempts at showing care for his children, but nothing came out of it. Now that the first is done with university, the second is in her final year and the last is in secondary school, he wants to come back fully into our lives.

As much as I will not stop my children from reconnecting with their father, there is no way we can be a family again. I have moved on and my children thankfully survived without a father so what do we need him for? Like I told him, if he is looking for a nurse, he should hire one. If he is looking for forgiveness, he should go to God. "

CHIBUEZE

"The decision to succeed is in our hands likewise the decision to fail. My parents did their best to train me up to secondary school level. After sitting for my SSCE(WAEC/NECO) exams two years ago, my father helped me to secure a job in his friend's business center where I work presently. He said his reason for helping me get the job is to enable me to have a source of income so as to save some money and use it to further my education. He planned for me to work for three years and save enough money from my salary because his friend told him that he would be paying 20, 000 naira monthly. My duties include helping people type documents and also do photocopy. He told my dad that he'd put me through in areas that I am experiencing some difficulties while carrying out my duties.

For the past two years, I have been saving 15,000 naira consistently every month out of my salary and supporting my parents with the rest for the upkeep of the home. I told my parents I don't think I would want to go back to school at the moment. This is because I'm looking at raising more money to purchase a photocopy machine and take it along with me to school by the time I gain admission into the university so that I will have a source of income while schooling. I don't want to leave all the burden for my parents to provide all my needs. They said it's a good idea, but I shouldn't worry because they'd see how they will support me. They said for now, I have to prepare my mind on going back to school from next year. I won't be happy that I would be quitting my job because my boss has been so nice to me. I was a novice, but he took his time to put me through in all aspects where I had difficulties and he was paying me even while I was learning. There was a day I asked him why he chose to treat me well and he said my father is his very good friend and the only way he feels he can repay my father's kindness towards him is through what he is doing for me at the moment. He was the person that gave me the idea of establishing a business center when I get back to school. I'm so grateful to God for using him to help me achieve all I have for the past two years and now. He is one of the reasons I believe that good people still exist and hopefully someday in the near future, I will also return this kind gesture he has shown towards me. "-

KINGSLEY

"When I got a visa to travel 8 years ago, my in-law was the first person I ran to for assistance to purchase a traveling ticket. Although he did not have money at that time, I knew him to be the type that would know people he can borrow from to assist me and I planned to pay back when I travel. He said he didn't have money and didn't know who to borrow from. I took all the money in my account and luckily for me, the airline was running a promo so I was able to purchase my ticket. I traveled and by the grace of God, I became successful.

In 2018, I visited Nigeria and went to see him at his spare parts shop. The shop was scanty of goods which I didn't like. He began telling me how hard things were for him and his family. I gave my aunt his wife money for food and promised to send money when I travel back for them to add to the business. I fulfilled my promise as soon as I traveled back. After some months, their daughter reached out to me on Facebook saying her dad sent her to tell me they had been issued a quit notice where they live. After asking how much a new place would cost and what they had, I sent money to support them.

In 2019, I visited Nigeria again and went to see them. I still found the shop in a bad state. When I visited another aunt, I told her what I saw and expressed my dissatisfaction. After the visit, this aunt called and told them what I said. My in-law interpreted it as me mocking him and went about telling others that I was mocking him. I was surprised because when I needed his help, he didn't help, but I have rendered help to him. I decided to cut off my relationship with his family. This was a man who didn't assist me in traveling, but had received assistance from me yet he is the one spreading false stories about me. When I heard that, I felt bad and decided to end my relationship with his family.

Recently, I visited Nigeria again, but this time around, I did not go to their shop. I believe there are some people that no matter how they pray or go to church, God doesn't answer their prayers because of the type of heart they have. People should know that God will not come down from heaven to help you, it is someone he will use to help you. People should mind what they say against others as it may turn against them. I would have continued to help them the best way I can but after the things they said, I will no longer help. "

CHUKS

"I have completely given up on this country called Nigeria. Daily, they keep looking for a way to frustrate her citizens by creating one useless policy or the other. I did my NIMC registration five years ago. I just recently got my NIN and the temporary card. When I went to immigration office to enroll for my international passport, I was told the date of birth on my NIMC is different from what I filled on the immigration form. I told them the mistake should be from NIMC because all my documents have 21st as my date of birth, but my National identity card has 31st. I can confidently say that the mistake is from NIMC. My passport enrolment was put on hold until I corrected the mistake. When I went to NIMC for correction, I was shocked when I was asked to pay 15,500 naira for the change of date of birth. At first I thought it was a joke until I logged into the site to generate the remita myself and I saw the same amount, I was short of words.

This country, especially this present government, has really frustrated 80% of Nigerians and it has made many people lose hope in this country. I don't blame those who left the country and vow never to come back or even those that risk their lives to flee the country through the sea and deserts. It's better to be a stranger in another land than be a stranger in your own country. It's high time we the citizens came together and speak with one voice. Let's say "No" to all these fruitless policies the government imposes on the citizens daily. I believe many people would have also faced the same problem I encountered and are scared to voice it out or some might just choose to bribe their way through."

IBRAHIM

"I can't say that it's by my power or because I'm special, but all I have to say is that it's by the grace and mercy of Allah that I'm alive today. Last Friday, I would have been dead and forgotten and I don't think my relatives would have been able to identify my corpse if I had died.

I narrowly escaped the fire incident that happened in Kubwa last Friday. I normally hawk my goods (okra and pepper) around where the incident happened. Usually, when they close the market,we stay back and sell to people coming back from work and those that usually come at night to buy what to cook. I was selling to one of my customers a few meters away from where the incident occurred.

The next thing we heard was a loud bang. I saw that a part of my trousers was on fire and the clothes of the man I was selling to were also on fire. We both ran and fell inside a nearby gutter thinking that there was water inside but there wasn't. I had no option than to try my best and remove my trousers and my top not minding that I was naked because I saw how the man also struggled to pull off his shirt so he won't get burnt and I did the same.

Immediately,people rushed to where we were and poured water on us. When they saw that we were fine, they went to where the fire broke out and were pouring water and doing their best to put out the fire. When I stood up and was trying to look for my wheelbarrow with my goods,I saw that it had been burnt completely. I saw many people that were burnt and people that died on the spot. People were screaming in pain. It was a terrible sight to behold. People really did their best before firefighters arrived with their truck. The police and road safety came too and were taking people to the hospital.

I don't think I would ever forget that day in my life. Each time I remember the incident, I feel so cold because some people died and their family don't even know where they were, they might think that they were somewhere else. Honestly, I really thank Allah for saving me using that customer that was buying something from me at that moment because I was actually pushing my goods heading towards that side,but I thank Allah for sparing my life.

NB:

THANKS FOR READING OUR STORIES.

ALL STORIES ARE PUBLISHED WITH THE CONSENT OF THE INDIVIDUALS.

WE'RE WORKING ON THE VOL2.

www.ingramcontent.com/pod-product-compliance
Lightning Source LLC
Chambersburg PA
CBHW070533220526
45467CB00003B/940